FROMELLES
THE FINAL CHAPTERS

Tim Lycett's lifelong interest in the First World War and his own historical research led him to establish the Fromelles Descendant Database, which works with the soldiers' relatives to help identify the lost diggers buried at Pheasant Wood. He was a Victorian crime-scene police officer for 25 years and now lives on the Gold Coast with his wife.

Sandra Playle is a genealogist with over 30 years' experience who worked closely with Tim and the other researchers on the identification of the soldiers. Her ancestors' service introduced her to Australia's military heritage, and she is committed to protecting the memory of this country's servicemen through many research projects. She lives in Pinjarra, Western Australia.

FROMELLES
THE FINAL CHAPTERS

How the buried diggers were
identified and their lives reclaimed

TIM LYCETT
and Sandra Playle

VIKING
an imprint of
PENGUIN BOOKS

VIKING

Published by the Penguin Group
Penguin Group (Australia)
707 Collins Street, Melbourne, Victoria 3008, Australia
(a division of Pearson Australia Group Pty Ltd)
Penguin Group (USA) Inc.
375 Hudson Street, New York, New York 10014, USA
Penguin Group (Canada)
90 Eglinton Avenue East, Suite 700, Toronto, Canada ON M4P 2Y3
(a division of Pearson Penguin Canada Inc.)
Penguin Books Ltd
80 Strand, London WC2R 0RL England
Penguin Ireland
25 St Stephen's Green, Dublin 2, Ireland
(a division of Penguin Books Ltd)
Penguin Books India Pvt Ltd
11 Community Centre, Panchsheel Park, New Delhi 110 017, India
Penguin Group (NZ)
67 Apollo Drive, Rosedale, Auckland 0632, New Zealand
(a division of Pearson New Zealand Ltd)
Penguin Books (South Africa) (Pty) Ltd
Rosebank Office Park, Block D, 181 Jan Smuts Avenue, Parktown North, Johannesburg 2196, South Africa
Penguin (Beijing) Ltd
7F, Tower B, Jiaming Center, 27 East Third Ring Road North, Chaoyang District, Beijing 100020, China

Penguin Books Ltd, Registered Offices: 80 Strand, London WC2R 0RL, England

First published by Penguin Group (Australia), 2013

10 9 8 7 6 5 4 3 2 1

Cover design by Nikki Townsend, copyright © Penguin Group (Australia)
Text design by Samantha Jayaweera, copyright © Penguin Group (Australia)
Cover photographs: The poppies photo is courtesy of Philippe Sainte-Laudy Photography/Getty Images. The soldiers' photos are courtesy of the Fromelles Descendant Database and the families of the soldiers' descendants.
The letter on page 214 is reproduced courtesy of courtesy of the National Archives of Australia
Typeset in Adobe Garamond 12.5/18.5pt by Samantha Jayaweera © Penguin Group (Australia)
Colour reproduction by Splitting Image, Clayton, Victoria
Printed and bound in Australia by McPherson's Printing Group, Maryborough, Victoria

National Library of Australia
Cataloguing-in-Publication data:

  Lycett, Tim, author.
  Fromelles: the final chapters / Tim Lycett; Sandra Playle.
  9780670075362 (paperback)
  Australia. Army. Australian and New Zealand Army.
  Corps–History.
  Fromelles, Battle of, Fromelles, France, 1916.
  World War, 1914-1918–Campaigns–France–Fromelles.
  World War, 1914-1918–Participation, Australian.

940.4272

penguin.com.au

Dedicated to the memory of

2719 Private Fred Lycett, 46th Battalion, AIF
6360 Private Victor Hill, 22nd Battalion, AIF
2809 Private Harold Day, 44th Battalion, AIF
1298 Gunner Edwin Austin, 106th Howitzer Battery, AIF

*Who numbered among the countless thousands of men destined
never to return home into the loving embrace of family.*

May they rest in everlasting peace.

Lest we forget.

THE MOTHER

Somewhere in France he lies-
Above his head the scarlet poppies blow,
And silver moons have bloomed and still will bloom;
Somewhere the distant great guns boom and boom-
And 'cross the Harbour blue, the wind with slow,
Sad whispers, sighs.

Somewhere in France he lies-
And I, I wailing, seek his empty room,
Stretching my arms out to the empty gloom,
Clasping a dream. Then through the day I go
With hollow eyes.

Somewhere in France he lies-
Oh hollow eyes, oh mouth that aches with woe,
No more for me shall moon or flower bloom-
And yet another, but less splendid tomb-
Ah, I am proud, am proud, to-day to know
In France he lies!

Somewhere in France he lies-
But oh, each scalding tear that dries
Upon my cheek; my moans, my cries,
That rise and still must rise
Up, up to Heaven and those cold blue skies!

Peter Austen (1892-1939)

CONTENTS

FOREWORD

The task of finding, recovering and identifying the young Australian soldiers who were slaughtered in France at the Battle of Fromelles has taken a great deal of effort from many people, all of whom have been unwavering in their commitment. The result is that many of the soldiers of Pheasant Wood have now been restored to their families, but in a far greater sense they have been restored to all of us. It is not blood specific; there is a collective ownership of their stories.

Certainly in the beginning, the journey was in need of support, and both Tim Lycett and Sandra Playle were integral to propelling it forward. Having entered the fray very early in the process, they advanced and enriched our research, and as the missing of Fromelles emerged from anonymity, both Tim and Sandra were there to help reveal them to us.

Weathering active discouragement and incredulity from the authorities that a burial site as large as Pheasant Wood could have been missed during post-war recoveries, the 'amateur' network persisted with Tim and Sandra in the vanguard, compiling a working list of burials, advancing our understanding of the men themselves and giving them a voice.

I acknowledge and thank them for their tireless volunteer work, for their skills and for their unfaltering application. In this book, they remind us that these soldiers had real faces and lived real lives, and of the importance of reinstating all our lost countrymen to their rightful place in Australia's conscience. The research and advocacy is continuous and ongoing, all in our common cause of commemoration and remembrance.

Lambis Englezos

Introduction
THE ATTICS OF OUR MEMORY

Remembrance restores possibility to the past, making what happened incomplete and completing what never was. Remembrance is neither what happened nor what did not happen but rather their potentialisation, their becoming possible once again.

From *Potentialities: Collected Essays in Philosophy* by Giorgio Agamben

This is not an in-depth history and analysis of the battle that took place at Fromelles, in northern France, in July 1916, as the strategies, tactics and leadership issues have already been covered by a number of other excellent works. Nor is the intention to simply relate biographies of the men killed and missing after the operation, although several of their stories are to be found in these pages. In essence, this book is about remembrance. It is about those who have championed its renaissance, those who have been impassioned by its re-emergence and those who have always held it dear.

Over the last thirty years, Australians have gained a new understanding of our nation's involvement in world conflict, resulting in our reconnection to the remembrance ethos that thrives today. 'Lest we forget' has a resonance that stirs people into action. Without this underlying motivation, the successful recovery of the bodies at Pheasant Wood may never have happened. In turn, the discovery at Fromelles has prompted many Australians to look deeper into their own family's past and to question what became of their ancestors who served and died in the Great War.

A strong motivation for writing *Fromelles: The Final Chapters* has been to explore the impact of loss on some of the relatives of the Fromelles missing and how the results of the findings have affected descendants nearly a century later. Equally important, though, is the fact that Fromelles has captured the imaginations and touched the hearts of many people who have no family ties to the tale. With a few notable exceptions, the main players in this narrative are not descendants or even distant relatives of the missing soldiers. I include myself in that group. Even so, we found ourselves pursuing recognition for these men with a fervour and commitment as if they were members of our own families. This, then, is also the story of the efforts of a network of genealogists and history buffs to research, locate and chronicle the missing men's lives and to restore them to us as fellow human beings, instead of inanimate figures locked within the attics of our memory.

The story of Pheasant Wood is populated with so-called 'amateurs', our work championed by the most celebrated Fromelles amateur of them all, Lambis Englezos. Behind the official histories and government reports is an army of volunteers with a vast range of skills, quietly contributing to the mass of information that was required to (literally) unearth the truth. Ordinary people feel connected to the quest through their participation in it, however small, whether it be a swab of DNA, a lucky purchase on eBay, the chance recognition of a face in the newspaper or spotting a familiar name while browsing the internet. Then there are the contributors such as myself, whose lifelong curiosity about a particular period in time inexorably drew us to the search.

For as long as I can remember, I have had a passion for learning about history. My personal fixation is the catastrophe that was the Great War of 1914 to 1918, and you don't have to go far to figure out what sparked my interest. Over four years, my grandfather Will Lycett managed to survive the fighting, from the landing at Gallipoli to Armistice Day on the Western Front. When I was still very small, he came to live with my family in the Melbourne suburb of Box Hill. As the youngest of five children, I was often left to my own devices and would wander into Pa's room for some quiet company. In my mind's eye, I see a small hand-tinted photograph of a young soldier gazing out of a yellowing frame on Pa's mantelpiece. I remember picking it up and asking him who it was. The old man turned to his inquisitive little grandson with glistening eyes and replied with a note of sorrow in his voice, 'That was my brother, Fred, who was killed in the war a very long time ago.'

Carefully replacing the photo, I went on my way, but the image of the young man stayed with me. I never ceased to wonder what had happened to him, but somehow I couldn't bring myself to ask Pa the circumstances of Fred's death. Even then,

I could sense a deep sadness that he was reluctant to talk about. It was only when clearing out my grandfather's cupboards after he died that we came across his wartime diaries, photographs and souvenirs. To a young teenager, these palpable links with the past were mesmerising, and they stirred the beginnings of what was to become an enduring fascination.

At school, I was an average student, except for the subject of History, at which I excelled. I went on to study it at university, but after one year the lure of financial independence was too strong, so I left to get a job as a quantity surveyor. Three years of stultifying office work sent me back to studying, and a new career in the police force, which I stuck at for the next twenty-five years.

Through it all, my interest in the First World War remained. I began to seek out stories of veterans like my grandfather and found myself focusing on the diaries of those who experienced its horror first-hand. I was always more captivated by the personal accounts of the soldiers than by the overall strategies and tactics of the conflict. I suppose this extended into my work as a police officer – constantly striving to uncover the story behind the face or the name.

As a natural progression, I started to research the lives of individual Australian soldiers and learned where to source a vast range of documents and files. Gradually, I began to assist others to connect with their families' wartime histories by helping them to understand more about what happened during their ancestors' periods of service. On many occasions, I found myself looking into the personal background of a particular soldier, painstakingly tracing where he fitted into the whole picture.

Genealogy played a major part in this. The nature of genealogy has shifted dramatically over the years. In the past, its primary focus was to determine the lines of kinship and descent of rulers and nobles. It was vital to be able to demonstrate the legitimacy of claims to wealth and power in the days when bloodline dictated social standing, particularly in Western societies. Then, in 1894, the Family History Library of the Church of Jesus Christ of Latter-Day Saints (also known as the Mormons) was founded to assist the brethren in tracing family lineages for special religious ceremonies that are central to their beliefs. It now houses the most extensive genealogical record-gathering program in the world.

These days, the practice of genealogy is far more widespread, with people from all walks of life exploring and documenting their family trees. The internet has revolutionised and popularised the subject, providing massive amounts of data as well as a means to share information and to educate the home 'dabbler'.

On the informal side, there are message boards where anyone can post a question about their topic and usually get some sort of helpful response. A great deal of generosity and goodwill goes into running these sites. For example, there is one called 'Random Acts of Genealogical Kindness' (RAOGK), which was set up with the express purpose of helping people who are researching far from home and are not able to travel. Whenever possible, the network will put them in touch with someone in the relevant location who will look up local records or take photographs on the applicant's behalf.

Online genealogical societies are more organised affairs and generally offer assistance in a unique area of interest, such as descendants with a particular family name, or from a specific part of the world, or whose ancestors took part in a significant historical event. Some of these sites are large enough to offer personal research assistance, newsletters, chat rooms, classes and seminars, and easy access to a wealth of useful records.

Facebook pages such as 'Australian Genealogy', 'Irish Roots Hunters' and 'British Isles Genealogy' are free to use and run by people who are happy to assist and love getting their teeth into a good mystery. 'Findmypast' and 'Ancestry and Genes Reunited' are paid subscription sites. 'Rootsweb' has free mailing lists and a message board, and the Mormon website is listed at www.familysearch.org. Such sites are invaluable resources and turn what can be a solitary pursuit into a hotbed of discussion and ideas.

My move towards genealogy also reflected a shift in my career. It's no secret that many police officers live for the adrenalin rush, although the old adage that law enforcement is 1 per cent excitement and 99 per cent paperwork is pretty accurate. For me, the thrill of the chase and the ability to seek out and combine evidence to reveal the truth were always the highlights of the job. Whenever possible, I would try to be among the first officers to respond to an incident, so I spent a lot of time on the road. As the years progressed, the imposed politics of police work were dragging me further and further away from the coalface, which was where I wanted to be. Luckily, before I hit burnout I was offered a position as a crime-scene officer, placing me right in the centre of the action.

At the same time, I started delving into family history on a more general basis. Blessed with an analytical mind, I was adept at finding even the most insignificant fact and piecing it into the framework of a family tree. I began corresponding with dozens of like-minded people, among them Sandra Playle, whose considerable range of genealogical skills complemented my own. A most rewarding partnership was born. Sandra and I collaborated on a number of intriguing projects, but nothing could have prepared us for the sheer scale of our hunt for the descendants of the soldiers buried at Pheasant Wood. Nor could we ever have predicted the emotional impact it would have on our lives.

It's my hope that this book will appeal not only to those who are already familiar with the Battle of Fromelles but also to people who know little about the catastrophe and want to understand more about how events of the past have influenced our lives today. To this end, we begin from the beginning, and the first part of the narrative is devoted to the operation itself. In the spirit of our work, I have endeavoured whenever possible to recount proceedings through the experiences of individual soldiers, so the reader can gain a sense of their unique journeys.

We then move to the contemporary section of the tale, when in 2002 a middle-aged schoolteacher from Melbourne entered the fray and ensured that a seemingly insignificant clash on the Western Front at French Flanders would finally emerge from the shadows of time. From this point on, the cast expands into a collective account that includes seasoned professionals, gifted amateurs and a host of passers-by who all played their part in helping to solve the puzzle. This book is very much their story as well.

There is a sense of urgency about the need to restore some humanity to the lost soldiers of Fromelles. For nearly a century, they were denied a proper burial and place of rest. Now that we can right the wrong, it seems only fitting that we tell the individual stories of how they came to be there. Unfortunately, in many cases there is little or nothing to work with in terms of archive material. But through diligent research and sheer luck, a growing number of men have begun to emerge from the obscurity of dusty files and precious old letters to tell us their version of what happened so long ago and so very far from home.

Chapter 1

ORIGINS OF THE LOST

And we wondered the while – when on History's page,
With Heroes' life-blood, their country's fame
Was lettered in fire, for each future age
To kindle ever in quenchless flame –
What honoured place in that glorious tale,
With their Nation's patriot Dead would share,
The comrades brave which Death's solemn veil
Left nameless, asleep in the silence there.

**Excerpt from 'Our Nameless Dead' by RQMS Thomas Brennan,
2nd Light Horse Field Ambulance**

Born in London in 1886, Robert (Bob) Courtney Green grew up with his brothers and sister near Sherwood Forest at Budby, Nottingham. Like millions of working-class men at the time, his father was in service, employed as the second butler to the Fourth Earl Manvers at Thoresby Hall.

After the eldest brother enlisted and sailed away to serve in the Boer War, the family suffered a great loss when Robert's father suddenly died after an operation in 1903. This no doubt placed considerable strain on the family's finances, and by 1908 Robert was working as a footman at Caversham, some 80 kilometres west of London. But a life in service did not appeal to Robert. He and his friend Bill Humann dreamed of adventure and set their sights on opportunities that were beckoning from the outer reaches of the Empire. In 1909 they boarded the mail steamer *Bremen* and sailed for Fremantle, Western Australia.

Upon arrival, the men took up temporary residence in a Perth immigrant hostel. They soon found labouring jobs and embraced the meagre existence of tent life in the Australian bush as they worked to clear the land. Despite the significant hardships and constant thoughts of home, Bob was relishing his new-found freedom and the chance it offered of independence. As he recorded in a letter home in 1913, 'Sometimes I think I would rather be in England, but it is the freedom, Mother, that appeals to me. We are our own masters and the equal of any man we meet along the road and that, as you know, is a great contrast to the old days.'

Eventually, the two friends saved enough money to purchase 250 acres of property, which they named Wundaleigh, in the gently undulating farming area around Bolgart, north-east of Perth. They worked hard to clear the land, planted their crops and began to make headway, with modest harvesting profits. But successive years of drought brought dispiriting losses and by 1914 the farm was in desperate trouble.

Fortunately for Bob, he'd found himself a happy diversion in the form of a young Scottish girl named Agnes Pearson, known to all as 'Nancie', who lived in nearby Toodyay. The two were often parted for considerable lengths of time while Bob slogged to make ends meet on the farm and Nancie pursued work as a nursemaid in Spencers Brook. Despite these protracted periods of separation, by the beginning of the Great War the couple had been engaged for some twelve months and were planning their future together.

With the outbreak of hostilities in Europe, Bob was ready to answer the call of his motherland and join up, but at the same time his obligations to Bill and the farm had to take precedence. Without him, the farm was bound to collapse, and he couldn't bear the thought of leaving his friend destitute, especially now that Bill was married with a young family.

In another letter written to his mother, in May 1915, Bob explained his position:

> The war has upset everything entirely and combined with it we have had a complete failure in the country with our crops. We ourselves didn't get 1/- return off of 250 acres cropped and as it takes between 3 and 4 hundred pounds a year to keep the place going you will understand that we have been thrown absolutely on our beams end. Just how we are going to fare we don't know yet, but when I tell you I have been navvying for the last 3 months and will be until after the next harvest (another 9 months) to keep us in food, you will see that we are hard pushed. Any idea of selling up is entirely out of the question now land can be had for a song. Our only chance is to try and struggle through in the hope of good seasons coming. But for the above it is very probable I should have been in Turkey now but I felt I could not go away and leave my partner to face it alone.

As news of the battles reached Australia, and the exploits of the Anzacs at Gallipoli were celebrated in the newspapers, the thought of being a 'stay-at-home' became too much for Bob. Two months after sending this letter, he parted company with Bill and enlisted with D Company, 32nd Battalion, Australian Imperial Force (AIF).

Embarking from Adelaide in November 1915 aboard HMAT *Geelong*, D Company comprised men almost exclusively from Western Australia. Their final training was conducted in the shadow of the Egyptian pyramids. It was here that Bob's evident maturity and leadership qualities were recognised, and he was swiftly promoted to the rank of corporal.

The camps in Egypt were flooded with old hands who had many tales to tell about their experiences in Gallipoli. No doubt, Bob and the other men of the 32nd Battalion listened intently to these stories, fuelling their impatience to prove themselves in battle.

By late June 1916, the wait was almost at an end. Landing in Marseilles, France, they collected their kits and marched with keen anticipation towards an entrenched German Army and their baptism of fire on the Western Front.

On the east coast of Australia, in early 1915, a sixteen-year-old Melbourne teenager attempted to enlist so he too could fight for his country. Discovered to be well under the legal age of eighteen, the young man was unceremoniously sent home, but his resolve was undiminished. And it seems his determination to join up at all costs was shared by his younger brother.

William Gordon was born in Port Adelaide, South Australia,

in 1899 and his younger brother John the year after in Carlton, Melbourne. Their mother was of pioneering South Australian stock and their father was an immigrant Scottish engineer. The boys had already left school and entered the workforce, helping to supplement the family's income as labourers and yardmen in the Carlton area.

William's failure to enlist did little to quench the two brothers' thirst for adventure. In July 1915, the boys fronted at different enlistment offices on different days. Both produced 'official' letters of consent from their parents and were duly accepted into the army. The two notes purportedly written by their father had dramatically different styles of handwriting, so it seems likely the brothers forged the notes for each other. Had they been produced on the same day at the same enlistment office, there may well have been questions asked.

Because of his previously unsuccessful attempt, William used the name of his younger brother John and was sent as reinforcement to the 2nd Division Signals Company. The real John then signed on a few weeks later, calling himself James Gordon, which was the name of a younger brother who had died in infancy several years before. The newly allotted 1130 Private James Gordon was then attached to D Company of the recently formed Victorian 29th Battalion and his appointment with the battlefield at Fromelles confirmed.

John's story was to become one of the most challenging to unravel ninety-odd years later.

Ignatius Bertram Norris was the youngest son of Richard and Marianne Norris. Christened as the namesake of Saint Ignatius, on whose feast day his birth fell in 1880, he was more commonly known to everyone by his second Christian name, Bertram, or simply 'Bertie'. Coincidentally, Saint Ignatius of Loyola just happens to be the foremost patron saint of soldiers.

Bertie was brought up in a devout Catholic family at Hunters Hill, Sydney. His father was a relatively affluent Sydney banker. When he was ten, Bertie was enrolled at Saint Ignatius College, Riverview. It seems he was not averse to taking risks: he nearly drowned when he threw himself in the school swimming pool even though he couldn't swim, and he later survived being run over by a dray. But he also proved himself to be strong of faith, an excellent academic student and a fine sportsman. He won prizes for Latin and English, competed with the debating team, and participated enthusiastically in rugby, cricket, tennis and golf. In later years, he was selected to play first-grade hockey for New South Wales.

Graduating with honours in 1896, he continued his association with Saint Ignatius College through the Old Boys' Union and served as its secretary in 1908. That same year, he was admitted to the New South Wales Bar as a barrister and simultaneously qualified as a solicitor, practising law with the firm of Messrs Brown and Beeby. He then went on to develop a flourishing general practice.

As a member of Australia's pre-war militia, Bertie had served with the New South Wales Irish Rifles before being promoted to major with the 34th Regiment Commonwealth Forces. This was the position he occupied when war broke out in 1914. On 1 March 1915, he applied for a commission in the AIF. In the same month, he married Jane Elizabeth (more commonly known as 'Bessie') Lane-Mullins.

In late June, accompanied by his wife, Bertie embarked on the HMAT *Ceramic*, bound for the training camps of Egypt. Upon arrival, he was appointed to command the 7th Training Battalion at Heliopolis, where he utilised his legal skills to preside over courts martial as judge advocate for those who committed infractions against discipline. By all accounts, he was a fair administrator of military justice.

Having his wife by his side in Egypt provided Bertie with an element of family life rarely available to the ordinary soldier so far from home. Unlike many men who were overseas when their children were born (and, of course, many men who did not survive to meet their children), in February 1916 Norris was fortunate to hold his newborn son, John Richard Bertram, in his arms.

However, he did not have long to enjoy the new state of fatherhood. Selected to command the 22nd Battalion, he promptly relinquished this to lead the newly formed 53rd Battalion. We don't know whether Bertie had any influence over this fateful appointment, but the 53rd Battalion just happened to be composed of men from New South Wales.

In June 1916, Bertie parted from Bessie and their little boy. He took the 53rd Battalion to France and Bessie took their child to England, where she waited anxiously for news of her husband on the battlefields of the Western Front.

In the 1850s a group of Mauritians sailed from their small African island nation to Australia determined to try their luck on the Victorian goldfields. The vast proportion returned to Mauritius empty-handed but some stayed and became involved in mercantile activities, exporting goods from their homeland to sell in the 'new' land.

Into this small community, Alfred Victor 'Vic' Momplhait was born in 1887. His father, Jean Baptiste Momplhait, had emigrated from Mauritius to work as a shipping clerk in Port Adelaide at the age of eighteen and there met the girl who was to become his wife. Edith Sawtell was the daughter of one of Jean's colleagues and only twelve years old when she first laid eyes on the man she would eventually marry. Her union with Jean never gained the approval of her staunchly Anglo-Saxon father and so they were forced to meet in secret until they eloped five years later, in 1883.

The couple had eight children during their twelve years of marriage, but only the eldest three survived childhood (Vic was the youngest). Jean died from consumption in 1895, leaving Edith to raise the children on her own. One can only imagine the grief she must have suffered in such a small window of time, losing five children and her husband in quick succession.

Growing up in Alberton, Port Adelaide, amid all the family tragedy and turmoil, Vic, his brother, Arthur, and sister, Clarice, all stayed on at the local school. Despite the inevitable taunts prompted by their foreign surname and dark complexion, they managed to receive a satisfactory education and Vic was singled out as a good all-round sportsman.

By the time he reached adulthood, Vic was a much-respected parishioner of Saint Paul Anglican Church in Port Adelaide, and he can be seen in several archival photographs enjoying the company of the congregation on community picnics. He obtained a position as clerk with the British Imperial Oil Company, a subsidiary of Shell Transport, at the Port Adelaide offices. Edith would have been proud.

With the onset of the First World War, Vic Momplhait enlisted on 17 June 1915 and was sent to recruit training at Keswick Barracks in Adelaide. He left Australian shores on the HMAT *Benalla* as a reinforcement with the 10th Battalion and arrived at Tel-el-Kebir, Egypt, where, after some shuffling of troops, he finally found a home with the 32nd Battalion and continued his training.

The 32nd Battalion arrived in France on 23 June 1916, and Vic and his fellow soldiers made their way to the Armentières front. It appears he did not have an easy time in the days leading up to the Fromelles engagement. On 7 July the battalion did gas-helmet training at Morbecque before moving to Estaires in preparation for the coming battle. Suffering from the effects of phosgene gas and dysentery, Vic was hospitalised at the 12th Casualty Clearing Station. He remained there for nearly two weeks before he was released back to his battalion the day before the battle.

It's not hard to surmise that Momplhait, full of exuberance and confident of victory, pushed for his release from hospital to enable him to join his mates for their first battle on the Western Front. With the gift of hindsight, we have to wonder if men like Vic would have been so eager had they had an inkling of the horror that awaited them.

Chapter 2

A WRETCHED, HYBRID SCHEME

Suggested first by Haking as a feint attack; then by Plumer as part of a victorious advance; rejected by Monro in favour of attack elsewhere; put forward again by GHQ as a 'purely artillery' demonstration; ordered as a demonstration, but with an infantry operation added, according to Haking's plan and through his emphatic advocacy; almost cancelled and finally reinstated by Haig, apparently as an urgent demonstration . . .

Charles Bean, official Australian war correspondent

Until the dedication in 2008 of the replica Cobbers statue at Melbourne's Shrine of Remembrance (the original being in the Australian Memorial Park near Fromelles), the name Fromelles did not appear on any memorial on Australian soil. The concept of Fromelles being a battle in its own right was studiously avoided by sources at the time, which referred to it instead as a 'raid', a 'feint' or a 'demonstration'. It looks like the powers-that-be did everything possible to downplay its devastating outcome as a way of safeguarding the morale of troops abroad and protecting the populace back home from the brutal realities of the conflict.

Included under the umbrella of the 1916 Somme campaign

(though some 80 kilometres distant), the first major engagement by Australian troops on the Western Front was destined
to languish in relative historical and national obscurity, over-
shadowed by the glories of Lone Pine, Pozières, Bullecourt,
Passchendaele and Villers-Bretonneux.

Straddling the Aubers Ridge, the town of Fromelles was a
valuable prize in possession of the German Army. The troops
defending it were made up of the 6th Bavarian Reserve (BR)
Division. They were certainly not the cream of the German
forces, but by July 1916 they were well experienced in trench
life and knew the area like the back of their hands.

Over many months, the occupiers had built a rabbit warren
of interlinked breastworks (tall barriers made of sandbags filled
with dirt, erected when the ground was too soggy to dig proper
trenches), which were approximately 1.2 metres high and 1.5
metres thick, with reinforced machine-gun pits placed at strategic positions. The trenches themselves had special pumps to
drain the boggy ground when rain turned it into a quagmire.
And huge reinforced concrete 'blockhouses' were built well back
from the front line. A haven for soldiers under bombardment,
they were so resilient that many of them still dot the landscape
today. It was a formidable defensive force.

The commander of the British XI Corps opposing it, Sir
Richard Cyril Byrne Haking, CBE, KCB, KCMG, had long
coveted the strategically advantageous heights the Ridge offered.
It was a mere 36 metres at its peak, but as the only prominent
position on an otherwise largely featureless terrain it presented
a tremendous strategic advantage for the occupiers. Haking

ultimately became known as the architect of the Fromelles plan. He had been rapidly promoted within the British Army during the course of the war due to the sudden swelling in its ranks and the severe losses that followed. He was a soldier of the old school of warfare, yet to grasp the emerging nature of modern battle. He maintained the outmoded stiff-upper-lip approach that said 'steadfast character and offensive spirit' were all that was required to overcome an enemy, regardless of superior numbers, fortified positions and massed defensive firepower. Referred to among his troops as the 'Butcher', Haking's inability to adapt to contemporary concepts – even after a similar plan he had devised using British troops against the Aubers Ridge in May 1915 had ended disastrously – saw him applying the same flawed principles when it came to the Fromelles battle in 1916.

The assault was primarily anticipated as a diversionary action to occupy the local German forces so that they wouldn't be transferred south to where the Somme battles were raging. However, the form of it changed repeatedly in the days immediately leading up to the confrontation.

In mid-June 1916 Haking proposed an attack upon the Sugarloaf Salient with a view to capturing a portion of the enemy trenches. Named after a sweet conical bread that was sold locally, the Sugarloaf had enormous strategic importance. On the flat Flemish landscape, this slight rise on the German front line had been transformed into a small fortress with a strong concrete bunker where machine-gunners were stationed. The fact that it also bulged slightly into no-man's-land made it an excellent vantage point over Allied positions. Gunners could shoot from the front as the Allies attacked, then continue shooting from the side if they passed by, and, if they made it further, they could shoot them from behind as they advanced into German territory.

Due to circumstances elsewhere on the Western Front, the plan to attack the Sugarloaf was temporarily suspended, but by early July, when it was believed that the German forces further south on the Somme might be weakening, it was put back on the agenda.

General Plumer, commander of the British 2nd Army, expanded Haking's plan with the idea of a complete break-through in the hope of joining up with the British forces on the Somme. When he suggested this to the leader of the British 1st Army, General Monro, who commanded Haking and his XI Corps, it then fell to Haking to revise his initial plan. Upon presenting it a few days later, it was turned down yet again.

On 13 July British General Headquarters (GHQ) once more ordered the action to go ahead but recommended it be scaled back to an artillery demonstration with a few small infantry raids if necessary. Monro, not satisfied with that idea, favoured Haking's original plan encompassing an infantry advance of three divisions, although he did stipulate that it must be limited to capturing only the German front line and support trenches.

The next day, Haking acknowledged the shortage of trained artillery and shells for the field guns and howitzers, necessitating a further alteration of the plan. He was forced to scale back the attack to only two divisions of infantry.

Around this time, General Sir James McCay, commander

of the newly arrived 5th Australian Division, got word that his brigades were to be attached to Haking and the XI Corps for the planned attack on 17 July. Even though he was aware that previous similar assaults over the same ground had failed dismally, McCay welcomed the news. The 5th Division was the last of the AIF to arrive in France from Egypt, and the prospect of being able to prove itself on this foremost stage of battle was gratifying.

Assembling his three brigade commanders, McCay outlined their course of action. The division was to attack on the left of the 61st British Division, the inter-divisional boundary falling across the Sugarloaf Salient. The 15th Brigade of the now legendary General Harold 'Pompey' Elliott would be on the right of the Australian line, next to the British division. In the middle would be Harold Pope's 14th Brigade, and on the extreme left would be Edwin Tivey's 8th Brigade.

Each brigade was to attack with two assaulting battalions in four waves, the first two waves being located in the front-line Allied breastworks and the second two forming up in the support lines to the rear. The remaining two battalions of each brigade were to form the reserve and man the front trenches after the assault had been launched. They would not be committed without Haking's approval, although an exemption was granted that half of one of these battalions could be utilised as carrying parties behind the fighting.

Preceding the engagement, a seven-hour artillery bombardment was scheduled to suppress the enemy's defensive capability and cut the barbed wire, enabling clear passage of approach to the German breastworks. This barrage was to intensify over the final three hours with several feigned 'lifts' (a tactic of suddenly ceasing the bombardment to make it look like the infantry were on the verge of attack) to entice the expectant German troops out of their bunkers, before dropping among them again.

Before preparations could commence in earnest, the fate of the battle was again up in the air. Elliott had spotted the inherent weakness in such hasty planning and plainly said as much to a British staff officer, who agreed with him. (Years later, Elliott would deliver a series of lectures on the Battle of Fromelles in which he scathingly referred to Haking's plan as 'a wretched, hybrid scheme' and 'a tactical abortion'.)

There were other voices of concern filtering through to the commander-in-chief at GHQ, Sir Douglas Haig. He considered the mounting apprehension but decided to proceed with the attack on the proviso that there was enough artillery to sustain the assaulting troops. At the same time, it was widely recognised that an attack on 17 July in this region was no longer a necessity, due to the latest favourable reports of German troop movements.

When Haking learned of these new circumstances, along with the possibility of postponement or even cancellation of the assault, he vehemently opposed the idea and maintained that the artillery was quite sufficient for the attack to succeed. With Monro's backing, Haking's resolute petitions were accepted, and life was once more breathed into the plan.

On 16 July Private Corigliano of the 32nd Battalion wrote a brief postcard to his father that was heavy with foreboding:

Somewhere in France
16 July

Dear Dad,

Just a line to let you know I'm well so far but things look dirty
ahead. I hope you get my pay alright. I wish I was just enlisting
now as all troops; well I suppose you know where they're going.
Oh well Dad, I say goodbye. Remember me to all at home.

I remain your affectionate Son,

Maurice

That same evening, the men of the 5th Australian Division
began making their way to their front-line positions in readiness
for the following day's attack. The arduous trek lugging supplies
and ammunition in the failing light took its toll on the men,
the majority of whom fell into an exhausted sleep upon arrival.

Fortune then smiled upon them, albeit temporarily, when
a heavy mist rolled in accompanied by a persistent drizzle.
Haking knew that the artillery would be ineffective in such conditions and postponed the barrage several times throughout the
night, pushing the start time further into the next day in the
hope that the weather would clear. Finally, in the grey morning light, he accepted that the attack could not proceed that
day and approached Monro for advice. The general's immediate reaction was to request a cancellation of the entire plan, but
by now Haig was determined that the repeatedly stalled assault
would go ahead, and it was duly rescheduled for 19 July.

The three brigade commanders set about withdrawing their
troops from the front line and reorganising them in preparation

for the ordeal to come. The men were granted time to rest in billets behind the lines, and many seized the chance to write letters and catch up on diary entries. Others enjoyed their final moments of respite in the local *estaminets* (small cafes). Despite the fact that less than half of the division had even seen the front line and most of them had only been there for two days, morale ran high among the troops. There was an atmosphere of quiet confidence that their courage and abilities would carry the day.

The reality was that this was a force with chronically inexperienced artillery. Effective bombardment to take out gunners and breach the forest of enemy wire was crucial to the success of those soldiers who had to physically storm the enemy lines, but they were relying on men who had only recently been converted from infantry and the light horsemen.

Another tremendous disadvantage was that most of the infantry had only vague ideas about the nature of trench warfare. Many were new recruits who had been deliberately sent to Fromelles – part of the area known as the 'Nursery' – because this was a relatively quiet location on the front where they could be initiated into the new form of protracted fighting. But within days they found themselves participating in a full-scale attack against the Germans.

One of the more sobering details that demonstrates how ill-prepared they were is the fact that only the first two waves of attackers were issued with protective steel helmets, while many of the soldiers in the third and fourth waves had to make do with their soft slouch hats. They simply didn't have enough supplies. It must have been a terrifying prospect for a soldier, to launch himself into a vicious storm of steel and lead without a decent form of head protection. No doubt, this would have contributed to the appalling casualty list.

In the lull before the storm, Major Geoffrey McCrae, commander of the 60th Battalion, found time to compose a poignant letter to his family. An architect from Hawthorn, Melbourne, the 26-year-old veteran of the Gallipoli campaign had been wounded twice on the peninsula and was well aware of the possible consequences facing both him and the men under his command. With maturity far beyond his years, he wrote:

> *Today I lead my Battalion in an assault on the German lines and I pray God that I may come through alright and bring honour to our name. If not I will at least have laid down my life for you and my country, which is the greatest privilege one can ask for. Farewell dear people, the hour approacheth.*

Just after midday on 19 July, the troops commenced filing through the communication trenches back to their assault positions. From the high ground of Aubers Ridge and the Fromelles church, German observers could clearly see the long lines of soldiers and equipment snaking their way forward. They were well aware that an attack was imminent and had been for quite some time. A sign above the German trenches taunted the Australians: 'ADVANCE AUSTRALIA – IF YOU CAN!' After it was shot away, it was replaced with 'Why so long? You are twenty-four hours late'.

Captain Alexander Ellis of the 29th Battalion eloquently described the move to the front:

From the line of lights a sound of rifle firing is heard and a spent bullet passes overhead with a pleasant, gentle sigh. Suddenly our feet strike a wooden flooring of some kind and we are swallowed up in darkness. We become aware, too, of a novel smell, a strong yet indefinable aroma which we find out later to be characteristic more or less of all trenches in all parts of the Western Front. It is a mixture of damp earth, high explosive, and perhaps of other things . . . The sounds of desultory rifle and machine gun fire are now loud and penetrating, and a burst of machine gun bullets sputters unpleasantly near us . . . A heavy black wall ten feet high lies before us. About us to right and left are ugly, shapeless masses of sandbags. Dug-outs. Between these, dim figures are moving, overcoats on, steel helmets in position . . . We look about us and see that a parados has been constructed a few feet behind the parapet. Both parapet and parados rise upwards from ground level, for here the country is much too damp for sunken trenches . . . This is the long awaited moment. Everybody is anxious to get on the fire-step and have his first peep over No-Man's Land. A succession of enemy machine gun bullets raps rhythmically along the top of the parapet.

As a response to the artillery barrage laid down by the Allies in preparation for the assault and the obvious build-up of troops behind their lines, the German artillery began steadily shelling the support lines and communication trenches.

To add to the confusion, the Australians' own artillery was causing mayhem in their front lines by persistent 'drop-shorts', particularly on the 8th and 14th Brigades. It took skill and experience to handle the large free-standing guns of the artillery. Positioned kilometres behind the actual battle, the gunners wouldn't see where their shells actually landed, just as the victims would never see the gun that wounded or killed them. Early in the battle, there would be a kind of practice run as the gunners shot at the target with their best guess. Armed with binoculars, observers closer to the battle would telephone back to let them know where the shell actually landed, and the gunner would adjust the gun barrel's angle and direction as well as the amount of charge required for the distance.

Much depended on the gunner's abilities; abilities that the recent arrivals simply hadn't had time to develop. Afterwards, those in the front line made bitter comments about shells that uselessly overshot the enemy or, far worse, fell short into their own lines, killing and maiming Allied soldiers. At this early stage, the casualties sustained from this 'friendly fire' were significant. Although demoralising, the Australian troops held fast, because it appeared the Germans were on the receiving end of a far worse hammering.

Corporal Hugh Knyvett of the 57th Battalion (recorded on his enlistment form as a 'Minister of Religion' from Moonee Ponds, Melbourne) recalled later:

We soon began to discover that the shells that were bursting among us were many of them coming from behind . . . Our first message over the phone was very polite. 'We prefer to be killed by the Germans thank you' was all we said to the battery commander. But as his remarks continued to come to us through the air, accompanied by a charge of explosive, and two of our officers being killed, our next message was worded very differently, and we told him that 'if he fired again we would turn the machine guns on to them'.

Despite considerable challenges and a number of early casualties, the Australian brigades all arrived at their appointed jump-off positions by 4 p.m. With still about two hours to wait, the men settled in and took what shelter they could find against the constant shelling. As the minutes ticked away, the reality of what lay beyond their trenches began to sink in. The Gallipoli veterans, though more accustomed to the sights and sounds of battle, could not possibly have anticipated the intensity of the Western Front, while the untested Australian reinforcements must have been shocked by its ferocity.

In his memoirs, *To the Last Ridge*, Walter Downing would later write of the Australians' initiation to Western Front warfare:

There was the frightful chaos of minenwerfers (trench mortars) shaking the ground into waves, trailing lines of sparks criss-crossed on the gloom, swerving just before they fell, confounding, dreadful, abhorred far more than the shells, killing by their very concussion, destroying all within many yards. The enemy knew that a division fresh to the Western Front was in the line. He was hell bent on breaking its spirit.

Elliott's men of the 15th Brigade had the greatest distance to cross no-man's-land. He placed the 59th Battalion on the right with a view to advance obliquely against the edge of the Sugarloaf Salient. Much depended on the preliminary bombardment taking out the Sugarloaf guns. A failure to do so would give free rein to devastating enfilade (gunfire from the flank directed along a trench or a formation of soldiers) across the front of the Australian advance.

The 60th Battalion was placed on the left of the 59th to attack alongside. As the area between the two front lines gradually tapered, so the distance between them closed. The men of the 60th did not have as much distance to cross, but they too might be subjected to fire from the Sugarloaf. In addition, both battalions were going to have to negotiate the Laies Brook, a channelled stream running diagonally across their front.

Held in reserve for the 15th Brigade were the 57th and 58th Battalions. Although not required to assault the German lines at the outset, the 58th Battalion would later be embroiled in one of the most futile aspects of the entire engagement.

Battalions of the 14th Brigade, commanded by Lieutenant Colonel Pope, held the centre of the Australian line. The 53rd Battalion had the more difficult task of crossing the widest stretch of no-man's-land from the brigade front. Although they were not required to capture the German strongpoint at Delaporte Farm, well behind the enemy front lines, they were still going to have to negotiate the deadly fire of 'Parapet Joe', a notoriously accurate German machine-gunner strategically positioned somewhere ahead.

Advancing in waves alongside them were the men of the 54th Battalion. With less than half the distance needed to cross no-man's-land from their line to the German breastwork, the 54th had a distinctly better chance of arriving there in one piece.

The boundary between the two assaulting battalions of the 14th Brigade was the Rue Delvas, a road that ran across no-man's-land and bisected the German front line almost precisely at the point where the two battalions would join and where the Australian Memorial Park stands today.

Manning the Australian line behind them as reserve and support were the remaining two battalions of the 14th Brigade, the 55th and 56th.

Of the four battalions belonging to the 8th Brigade under Brigadier General Tivey, the 29th and 30th maintained a support position, while the attack was launched by the 31st on the right and the 32nd on the left. These battalions were to penetrate the German lines and push on to capture the German strongpoint at Delangre Farm, moving as far east as the Kastenweg, a major enemy communication trench that ran from the front line directly to the rear of the German position. These battalions primarily consisted of rugged miners and tough bushmen. They had the least distance to cover across no-man's-land and would not easily be denied their goal.

As 6 p.m. approached, troops on both sides braced themselves for battle. The men stood to and awaited the signal. Over the next twenty-four hours, the darkest chapter in Australian history – forged in the blood of its youth – would be written.

Chapter 3

THE DARKEST NIGHT

It was our first night in the trenches,
The parapets were red,
The duckboards they were covered
With our wounded and our dead
Across 'No-man's Land' we doubled,
How was it done I cannot tell,
For the guns they loudly thundered
'Twas like a blazing hell.

Men of the 29th Battalion, October 1916
Edwin Tivey's 8th Brigade

Four days before the battle, Bob Green, of the 32nd Battalion, 8th Brigade, cabled his beloved fiancée, Nancie, to wish her many happy returns for her birthday. On the morning of 19 July, he scribbled a quick postcard letting her know he was 'still going strong'.

At 5.53 that same afternoon, Bob Green, Vic Momplhait and the other men of the 32nd Battalion climbed the breast-work and began to make their perilous way towards the German lines.

On the 8th Brigade's front, casualties began to litter the field as the Australians advanced, many officers among them. As the first waves negotiated the barbed wire and approached the enemy's parapet, soldiers of the Bavarian regiment appeared to retreat. Except for a few pockets of resistance, by the time the Australians entered the trench enemy troops were running back across the open ground beyond. Clearing the frontal system and its dugouts of stubborn defenders commenced in earnest.

Thirty-six-year-old Brisbane wharf labourer Percy Weakley, of the 31st Battalion, epitomised the spirit of these first Australians to breach the enemy lines. A husband and father, Weakley had a somewhat chequered career following his enlistment in July 1915. He was 'crimed' twice for being absent without leave while training in Egypt, and less than a week before entering the fray at Fromelles he was found guilty of drunkenness.

It was the heat of battle that displayed the true mettle of Private Weakley the soldier. Upon seeing a German machine-gun crew beating a hasty retreat, he leapt over the parapet and took on the lot of them single-handedly. The Germans were unprepared for this brazen assault and Weakley accounted for four of them in quick succession. He probably would have despatched them all had he not been cut down by shrapnel and killed.

Following their successful assault on the front line in the 8th Brigade sector, the subsequent waves of Australians pushed further into the grassland beyond, looking for the German second- and third-line breastworks that had shown up on aerial photographs taken before the battle. But these 'lines' on the photos had been misinterpreted, and their objectives simply did not exist. Where their sketch maps indicated further enemy

trenches, they found nothing more than a series of water-filled
drainage ditches. Realising they had no hope of penetrating further without accurate information and support, the 31st and
32nd Battalions began digging in along the ditches.

Across on the left, Bob Green and D Company of the
32nd had pushed on and seized about 140 metres of the
long Kastenweg communication trench up until just short of
Delangre Farm. They did not know that the orders to capture
this German strongpoint had been withdrawn from the plans
prior to the attack, and news of the alteration reached them too
late. Bob's platoon commander, 2nd Lieutenant Samuel Mills
(a miner from Kalgoorlie, Western Australia), had already been
wounded twice but continued to command his troops to block
and hold the Kastenweg with a machine gun and grenade-like
hand bombs.

A handful of scouts were sent out in front to screen the 8th
Brigade positions. Among them was a young brass moulder
from Adelaide, Harold Jose of the 32nd Battalion. Crawling
forward of the Australian line, Jose was picked off by a German
sniper and lay wounded and paralysed. His fifty-year-old comrade Thomas Hunt went out to give assistance. As he tended
to Jose, Hunt himself was wounded, but he continued to dress
the young lad's injuries. Then, hoisting him over his shoulders,
he headed back towards safety. Wounded again before reaching
the Australian trench, Hunt stumbled to his knees, but he managed to get back on his feet and gathered Jose in his arms. Once
more staggering towards shelter, the gallant Hunt was barely
10 metres from sanctuary, the stricken Jose still in his arms,

when a single bullet tore through the chests of both men, killing them instantly.

By now, the enemy shelling had increased and was taking its toll. In a horrible irony, the Australian artillery further back continued to drop shells that fell short, killing and maiming their own men. German machine-gun fire raked the ground, and the number of casualties steadily climbed.

Corporal Theo Pflaum later recalled his personal experience in a diary entry:

> He [Captain Marsden] *told me that our fellers wanted help in the German lines and asked me if I could take a gun and tear across at once to work on my own initiative and to do my best. Will I ever forget that rush for life? The ground we covered was one mass of explosions and the shrapnel bursting above us and the flares continually going up lit up the whole place as bright as daylight. Time after time I fell, got hooked up in the barbed wire or fell into a shell hole but each time managed to scramble together and start again. At last we reached their trench and although I was exhausted, took a gulp for joy when I saw the other fellers behind me coming in one by one until the lot arrived. A lucky six we were.*

The companies of the 30th Battalion, intended to carry stores and equipment between the lines, were now unofficially drawn into the fighting to help bolster the defensive line. Preparing for inevitable counter-attacks, the Australians of the 8th Brigade didn't have long to wait.

Dusk heralded the beginning of the end. The first German counter-attack struck the 32nd Battalion's left flank and the call went out for reinforcements. The 30th Battalion was ordered to assist but, as a large proportion of that division had already been ensnared in the fighting, there were not many left to send. Small bands of soldiers from the 30th who were still available for support arrived with supplies and ammunition. They found exhausted men desperately defending their position along the Kastenweg. In front yawned an ever-widening gap between the 31st and 32nd Battalions, manned only by dead and wounded, and the reinforcements rushed to fill it. With heroic determination and sustained machine-gun and rifle fire, the Australians managed to hold off the Bavarians, but only just.

It was at about this time that Bob Green's luck finally ran out. Fighting to hold the Kastenweg at its advanced point, he was badly wounded in the chest by flying shrapnel. Even though he lay on open ground, two members of his platoon went out to bring him in. Private Percy Allengame was killed in the attempt, and Lance Corporal Allan Bennett, a grocer from Kalgoorlie, was hit in the spine as he carried Bob to safety. Both still alive, Bob and Bennett were dragged back into the Australian position and made as comfortable as possible.

Sergeant Walter Flindell of D Company recalled of Bob four months later, 'He was lying wounded next to Bennett in the German second line which we attacked from Fromelles. He was "pretty bad". I spoke to him and gave him a drink. I think he was hit in the shoulder.'

By 11.30 p.m., as the number of defenders dwindled with

each passing minute, more support arrived in the form of A and D Companies of the 29th Battalion. They had been released before authorisation from headquarters, but as their commander, Lieutenant Colonel Clark, explained, 'there was no other option'. Included in D Company was John Gordon, the underage yardman from Carlton, Melbourne.

With the two companies of the 29th Battalion now committed to the battle and its two remaining companies left to garrison the original Australian front line, the 8th Brigade had finally exhausted all its reserves. Meanwhile, on the other side of the line, the Germans had committed only a small number of theirs.

At 2.30 a.m. the Bavarians again attacked the advanced Australian line in front of the 31st Battalion. Swamping the outpost screen, they opened up a gap that allowed the right side of their forces to pour past the remaining pocket of Australian defenders into their old front line. From there, they swept towards the Kastenweg, scything through the men of the 29th Battalion as they went.

Barely three hours after he was hastily thrust into his first action, the young John Gordon fell in a hopeless attempt to defend the ground won by his countrymen. As much a victim of poor planning as he was prey to an aggressive German counter-attack, in the wider scheme of Western Front brutality his death went by unnoticed.

At this point, the remaining advanced parties of the 8th Brigade realised that the Germans were reoccupying their former front line behind them. With pressure mounting before them, they had to accept that there was no longer any chance of salvaging their position. Lieutenant Mills at the Kastenweg barricade passed the word along that, at the given signal, all those who were able should turn and rush the enemy in the German breastwork behind them and from there make their way back across no-man's-land to the comparative safety of their original front-line trenches. This meant it was impossible to carry out the wounded, so Bob Green, Allan Bennett and the rest would have to be left behind. No doubt, there were painful scenes between mates as the able-bodied bid farewell to their fellow soldiers too incapacitated to save themselves.

At 3.45 a.m. the surviving 150 members of the 8th Brigade made their mad dash for safety. Machine guns opened up on them from all angles, extracting a vicious toll as the men desperately clawed their way back through the reoccupied German front line before crossing the bullet-swept fields of no-man's-land. In an action that was seen as typical of the Australians, when a couple of soldiers were captured by the Germans in the front line, several of their mates up ahead turned back and freed them with an old-fashioned bout of fisticuffs.

Only a few straggling remnants of the brigade managed to regain their line. For those who had not heard the order to retire and those lying wounded, including Bob Green, John Gordon, Allan Bennett and Vic Momplhait, the end came quickly. They were all either captured or killed, although their individual fates would remain a mystery for many years to come.

Of Vic Momplhait, still very little is known. There is no account of where, when or how he was killed other than a brief reference in a letter home by an officer of B Company: 'You no doubt have heard of a "little raid" which our division carried out a fortnight ago. It was cruel and I'm not going to describe it. Vic Momplhait was killed. He was in our company. Poor beggar is in Fritz's trenches somewhere.'

Fortunately for Bob Green's family, Nancie made a frantic request to the Red Cross, and they in turn made direct enquiries among the men who had been with him and survived. Although not able to provide a definitive answer about his fate or offer any real solace to his loved ones, the responses enabled them to piece together the final moments before he was left to the mercy of the approaching Bavarian soldiers. Of these, the most helpful description comes from Lieutenant Mills, who was later awarded the Military Cross for his actions during the battle:

> He was in my platoon and wounded pretty severely on the night of 19/20th July. With the help of two other men we carried him to a place of comparative safety and dressed his wound. This was 200 yards behind the German first line and it was found impossible to get stretcher bearers through the barrage. When the order to retire was given it was a matter of charging through the two lines of Germans and so impossible to carry badly wounded men. Green was left with some twenty or thirty others some of whom have since been reported as prisoners. It is my opinion that Corporal Green died of his wound although he was alive when I saw him last. His behaviour was beyond praise and I have never seen a braver man. I always placed great reliance in him and it was amply justified.

POMPEY ELLIOTT'S 15TH BRIGADE

Brigadier General Harold 'Pompey' Elliott had voiced his reservations about the Fromelles plan from the outset. He was deeply reluctant to send the men of his 15th Brigade. Despite his doubts, though, when the moment came he bolstered their confidence and assured them of complete success:

> *I am writing this in the morning and about 6 o'clock this evening we will start a battle. Nothing like what is going on down on the Somme, but in other wars it would be a very considerable battle indeed. I have taken every precaution I can think of to help my boys along, and am now awaiting the signal which will launch so many of my poor boys to their death. They are all eagerly awaiting the signal, and we hope to pound the enemy's trenches that we won't have much loss at all . . . I am going to watch the assault from our front line. I cannot stay back here.*

By the time it was all over, he was reduced to tears.

On the right of the Australian attack, the 15th Brigade was directly facing the deadly Sugarloaf. With the widest distance to cross to reach the enemy, the first waves of the 59th and 60th Battalions 'hopped the bags' at 5.45 p.m. – a full fifteen minutes before their artillery barrage was due to lift off the German line. Following them at five-minute intervals were the remaining three waves of assaulting troops. Aiming to quash any resistance from the Sugarloaf strongpoint and destroy the front trenches, the men of the 15th Brigade watched the artillery onslaught prior to the assault as it pounded the enemy positions. Buoyed by what appeared to be a crushing display of power, their confidence soared. Even Pompey Elliott was heard to impress upon those nearby in the front line, 'Boys, you won't find a German in the trenches when you get there.'

As the second wave left their trenches, the sharp report of musketry reached their ears through the roar of the bombardment. When the third wave left, a single machine gun was heard to open up from the Sugarloaf. Finally, just after the last wave of the 15th Brigade attacked, the barrage lifted, and what had initially been a desultory reaction from the enemy suddenly increased to a shattering crescendo of rifle and machine-gun fire. The Germans had merely been biding their time.

Observers reported to Elliott occasional glimpses of the 59th and 60th Battalions continuing to advance across the wasteland, steadily approaching the enemy trenches. Minutes later, the cacophony of battle died down, and it seemed the Australians must have reached the German line and driven the enemy from it. In the absence of news to the contrary, a somewhat relieved Elliott reported that the attack appeared to be successful. His optimism was short-lived.

Soon after, runners (soldiers charged with the task of passing on messages from one area of command to another) and wounded began straggling back with news of the unfolding catastrophe. Major Herbert Layh, second-in-command of the 59th Battalion, described how his men had been unable to penetrate the German front line and were holed up in no-man's-land. Other reports reached Elliott that the 60th had breached the line but urgently needed support as their numbers were so depleted. He immediately ordered the 59th to make another attempt, unaware that its command structure had been almost completely wiped out. Only a handful of men were still standing as the majority were lying dead or wounded across the breadth of no-man's-land.

The entire 15th Brigade attack had been shattered right across the front. Although some small pockets of men appear to have reached the German parapet or possibly even entered the enemy line, they were so few in number that they were swiftly overwhelmed.

Before long, the horror of the situation became apparent to Elliott, and he immediately sent a message to his divisional commander, General McCay: 'The trenches are full of the enemy. Every man who rises is shot down. Reports from wounded indicate that the attack is failing from want of support.'

The truth of the situation was that they never had a chance.

When the first wave of Australians braved no-man's-land, they were met with sporadic rifle fire. Then a lone machine gun opened up on them as they negotiated the wire. It appears that a handful of Germans had been prepared to endure the hail of artillery and stand firm in their firing line so as to warn their comrades sheltering in dugouts of an approaching raid.

The 60th Battalion on the left of the attack negotiated the Laies Brook without incident, as it was only about half a metre deep in most places, but as it ran diagonally towards the Sugarloaf on the right, the troops began gravitating in that direction. The 59th on the right had also begun the advance relatively intact, an area of broken ground shielding them from the Germans' view. But as the leading waves of both battalions reached the halfway point across no-man's-land and cleared their respective shelters, they found themselves out in the open, virtually sitting ducks to the ceaseless enfilade from the Sugarloaf.

In a crucial error, the Australians assumed the machine-gunners stationed in the German salient had been pounded into submission by the artillery. In fact, most of them had withstood the battering by seeking refuge in their deep dugouts. The moment the barrage lifted, these men returned to their positions and opened up a withering fire on the Australians. Similarly, on the German front line, the Bavarian infantrymen poured back into the trenches from their safe havens and began a fusillade of relentless rifle fire at the advancing waves.

Closest to the Sugarloaf, the 59th Battalion was first to be cut down by the deadly hail of bullets. The line virtually melted into the ground and was annihilated. The 60th Battalion fared a little better, managing to reach the German wire, a few men even reaching the German parapet and front line. Like the 59th, though, the battalion soon disintegrated.

Private Harold Montague Nitchie was one of those 60th Battalion men to reach the enemy line. Fondly known as 'Monty', Harold was the youngest of six brothers to enlist from Geelong, Victoria. In an extraordinary coincidence, amid the bullet- and shrapnel-swept landscape of no-man's-land, Monty happened across his brother, James. The 60th would have started out close to its full complement of 1000 members. Nearly 400 were killed in the advance, countless more were wounded and many of those still standing sought refuge in no-man's-land, unable to move forward or backward. Against the odds, these two brothers were among the pitifully few who made it to the German front line.

We can only imagine what passed between them as they shook hands while the battle raged around them. And then, shockingly, a shell exploded close by, mortally wounding James. Cradling his brother as he slipped away, Monty would have suffered an unimaginable anguish when soon afterwards he was forced to retreat, leaving his brother's body to the mercy of the Germans.

The task of writing home to his brother's wife and children, telling them of the loss of their husband and father, must have been distressing to say the least. And yet, in a strange way, the Nitchies could be considered fortunate, because for them there was never any doubt about the fate of their loved one.

There was no saving the following three waves from destruction. Advancing behind the first, the second was ravaged as soon as the men left the trenches and ground entirely to a halt about halfway across. The third, thinking the first two waves would be lying off the German line, preparing for a final assault, pushed forward but was likewise demolished. The defending Bavarian regiment must have been amazed to see a fourth and final wave of Australians make a hopeless attempt to seize their trenches, but without hesitation they duly obliterated it like the rest.

Sergeant Walter Downing of the 57th Battalion, watching the carnage unfold from the support line, later described what he saw:

Scores of stammering German machine guns spluttered vio-
lently, drowning the noise of the cannonade. The air was thick
with bullets, swishing in a flat lattice of death. There were gaps
in the lines of the men – wide ones, small ones. The survivors
spread across the front, keeping the line straight . . . Hundreds
were mown down in the flicker of an eyelid, like great rows of
teeth knocked from a comb.

Corporal Hugh Knyvett, the minister from Moonee Ponds who
ended up writing an outstanding account of his wartime experiences, recalled the events with tragic precision:

The first wave went down like wheat before the reaper. When
the time came for the second wave to go over there was not a
man standing of the first wave, yet not a lad faltered. Each
gazed at his watch and on the arranged tick of the clock leaped
over. In many cases they did not get any farther than the first
wave. The last wave, though they knew they had to do the work
of three, were in their places and started on their forlorn hope at
the appointed moment.

When the barrage finally lifted, those left of the 59th Battalion,
knowing they had no hope should they remain where they
were, made a final desperate lunge for the German trenches.
Most died almost the instant they rose, others on the German
wire. However, one group containing Private Thomas Cosgriff,
a twenty-year-old printer from Melbourne, did manage to make
it to the enemy parapet and engage in direct combat. But the

futility of their efforts was a foregone conclusion, and the valiant Cosgriff was never heard from again.

As evening drew to a close, the pitiful remnants of the two battalions began to burrow into depressions and agricultural furrows in the ground in a vain attempt to protect themselves from the merciless shower of lead.

Alongside the 15th Brigade, the British 61st Division also made an assault on the German line. In almost a mirror image of the Australian attack, elements of the British forces managed to capture the German frontal system, but when the 184th Brigade came up against the Sugarloaf, it too failed dismally.

In charge of this brigade, Brigadier General Carter arranged with his divisional headquarters to concentrate their artillery on the Sugarloaf until 9 p.m., after which they would attack it again with available reserves. Shortly before 8 p.m. he sent a message to Elliott briefly outlining the plan and requesting cooperation in the form of a combined assault. Having just had his two reserve companies of the 58th Battalion released to him by General McCay, Elliott ordered them to prepare for a renewed attack against the east face of the Sugarloaf while the British assaulted the western side.

In the meantime, upon reviewing the British position, Haking decided they would pull back to the original starting position and regroup. Therefore, the attack on the Sugarloaf was cancelled and a message to this effect sent through to McCay's divisional headquarters at 8.35 p.m. In what can only described as an appalling bungle (if not criminal negligence), it was not until 9.25 p.m. that McCay forwarded notification of Haking's order to Elliott: '61st Division not attacking tonight. General Elliott may withdraw 59th Battalion and its reinforcements if he thinks attack is not likely to succeed.'

By the time he received the message, Elliott was helpless to prevent the slaughter. By then, the 22-year-old Duntroon graduate Major Arthur Hutchinson had already left the trenches with his two companies of the 58th Battalion and they were making their way across the fields. Picking up survivors of the 59th Battalion on the way, C and D Companies advanced towards the waiting enemy machine guns. They believed they were part of a two-pronged attack, with their British Allies advancing on the right. But they were on their own.

When the Australian line was two-thirds of the way across, the Germans unleashed a deafening hail of fire. Staggering under the impact, the attackers buckled and disintegrated in one of the most futile episodes of the entire Fromelles battle.

For Pompey Elliott's 15th Brigade, it was over.

HAROLD POPE'S 14TH BRIGADE

The first wave of the 14th Brigade's 53rd and 54th Battalions began their advance in the middle of the Australian line at 5.43 p.m. They made relatively steady progress despite suffering numerous casualties from artillery fire.

The right of the assault line was temporarily stalled by enfilade fire from the German front that should have been accounted for by the 60th Battalion, but once joined by their second wave it advanced, entering and clearing the enemy breastworks. Everywhere else along the 14th Brigade's front, the leading wave reached the German trench just as the barrage lifted and the Bavarian troops were emerging from their dugouts. Desperate hand-to-hand fighting ensued, but the determined Australians seized the line and consolidated.

The action was apparently progressing well. The construction of a communication trench began across no-man's-land from the Australian front, and machine guns were sent over with the 14th Machine Gun Company. But matters started to unravel and confusion set in quickly.

Commanding the 53rd Battalion, Ignatius Norris crossed no-man's-land with the fourth wave. Determined to continue the momentum beyond the captured first line, he led the way shouting, 'Come on lads! Only another trench to take!' Eyewitness accounts tell that he had just climbed over the parapet when he was killed by machine-gun fire. His adjutant, Lieutenant Harry Moffitt, an accountant from Bendigo, Victoria, attempted to bring Norris in with several others but died in the process.

In a letter written to Norris's grieving wife in England, the battalion padre, Father John Kennedy, wrote:

> *Your dear husband died a hero's death, leading his battalion in an engagement on the 19th inst. God knows how I pity you — but you have the great consolation of knowing that the Colonel was prepared to die . . . and you will be able to tell your child later how brave his father was, and above all how noble and conscientious a Catholic.*

Soon afterwards, Major Victor Sampson, the commander of C Company and veteran of the New Guinea expedition early in the war, also fell. Badly wounded about 9 metres beyond the German first line, he asked his men to arrange his broken body so he could assist them by throwing bombs. It was the last time he was seen alive.

At some point, anonymous hands salvaged Sampson's binoculars from the battlefield and carried them throughout the fray and back to safety. In the coming months, they were traded between soldiers until they eventually wound up in the possession of a 30th Battalion soldier, 3996 Private William Arthur, who had arrived in France four months after Fromelles. Arthur took them back to Australia and used them for the rest of his life to watch the races from the loft window of his Trafalgar Street home in Annandale, Sydney, which overlooked the Harold Park trots. It was only in 2010, after many years of searching, that William Arthur's nephew, Paul Arthur, obtained enough information to contact the grateful family of Victor Sampson and return the binoculars to their rightful owners.

With the company commanders, their deputies and six platoon leaders all casualties, the leadership structure of the battalions was in tatters. Command of the 53rd now fell to the 21-year-old Duntroon graduate Captain Charles Arblaster. In the 54th, the only remaining senior officer was its commander, Lieutenant Colonel Walter Cass.

The battalions pushed on regardless into the ground beyond the German breastwork, looking for the non-existent second and third defensive lines. Like the 8th Brigade, they could not locate them. By the time it was realised that there were no defence systems, the advance was thinning and had become hopelessly scattered.

Pulling what men they could back to a series of shell holes and ditches, Arblaster and Cass took up defensive posts on either side of the Rue Delvas, the road that bisected the battalions. On Arblaster's right, where the 60th Battalion was supposed to be, the line was forced to bend back to the German front line to protect his flank. It was here that the Germans mounted their first counterattack.

They pressed in on the Australian advanced posts and mounted a push along their old front line, which was now only sparsely held by the Australians (most of whom had moved on into the advanced defensive line). Clearing what troops had stayed behind, the Germans threatened to cut off the Australians, but in the nick of time Captain Norman Gibbins and two companies from the 55th Battalion in reserve stormed forward into the trench and repelled the attack before moving out to support the advanced positions.

Undeterred, the Germans continued to apply pressure on Arblaster's right along their old front line. A dogged defence mounted by the Australians thwarted them, but gradually, as the number of defenders dropped away, they were forced to give ground. It wasn't long before the enemy had reclaimed a substantial length of their original breastwork and were edging behind the right of the advanced 53rd Battalion line. By then, even they were exhausted.

3545 Sergeant John Gotch Ridley, 53rd Battalion, was

the son of Thomas Ridley of the famous Melbourne publications distribution company Gordon and Gotch. Shot through the neck, he remained conscious during the ordeal and later recorded in his notebook this vivid description of the battlefield:

> As I lay in McDonald's arms gasping for breath and very faint, I had a terrible scene of war before me. I had seen many pictures of war, now I saw it in all reality. The dirty, muddy ditch was tinged with scarlet round my body – this was my own blood; to my right lay a couple of men, one of them was Lawson dead and the other kept groaning. Just in front was a poor chap stuck in the mud and he was pulled out by Elliott. Right in front and on either side were dead bodies and groaning men. Some poor fellows who could walk passed us trying to get to the rear. Blood was everywhere. I heard many cries and groans of agony and the name of 'Jesus' and 'God' were constantly uttered. It was awful – a Christian land, two Christian nations and they made a part of God's earth a Hell. One wondered in his pain and agony, where was the glory of war.

Ridley was carried from the field by two soldiers and, despite the severity of his wounds, he survived that day. He returned to action, was later promoted to lieutenant and was awarded the Military Cross in 1918.

Around midnight, in an amazing feat of endurance, the communication trench across no-man's-land was completed by the 14th Engineer Company. In total, it was approximately

180 metres in length. It had taken 120 infantrymen and forty sappers to dig it, and forty infantrymen to carry in duckboards and bags.

Shortly after 1 a.m. the Germans redoubled their efforts behind and in front of the 53rd Battalion. A furious bomb fight ensued, as more and more of the remaining Australians were drawn in to defend their position. But the German advance was inevitable, and before long they had reoccupied the line up to and including its intersection with the Rue Delvas. From there, they were able to fire into the back of the 53rd Battalion posts. Knowing his position was now untenable, in a last-ditch effort Arblaster ordered his men to charge the Germans to the rear. As they rose, they were slammed with a barrage of gunfire and instinctively recoiled into their furrows. Arblaster himself was badly wounded in this attempt and died in a German military hospital several days later. The crushed survivors crawled over the Rue Delvas and into the 54th Battalion's lines.

As dawn approached, Cass accepted that the situation was hopeless. He got word through to divisional headquarters outlining the critical state of affairs and was advised to prepare for a retirement. Cass instructed Gibbins to organise a rearguard, but by doing so and pulling his men back to the small portion of the German front line that they still held, he left a gap in the advanced line that allowed the Germans to penetrate behind Cass's position.

It took eight runners to relay the message. One by one, they were killed, wounded or went missing, so it wasn't until 7.50 a.m. that Cass received the order to retire. With Germans now streaming through the gaps in the line, the word spread to use the newly constructed communication trench wherever possible while Gibbins and his rearguard held off the pressing enemy. Progress was slow, but many men had the 14th Engineer Company to thank for their survival. Those not in a position to access the trench chose to strike out on their own or stay put and fight it out.

Herbert 'Nutsy' Bolt was one of those trying to make it back that morning. A renowned rugby star from Newtown, Sydney, Nutsy was a rugged, brawling utility back who had represented his state on at least two occasions, playing alongside the famous Dally Messenger. Only after Nutsy's team was finally eliminated from the City Cup in 1915 did he bid farewell to his wife and daughter and enlist.

As Nutsy approached the communication trench, the Germans moved in to attack. In true Bolt style, he took to them with bayonet and rifle butt, accounting for at least six before a bullet smashed through his head, ending his life.

For the 14th Brigade, the battle had raged for over twelve hours. They had held out the longest, and no ground was gained.

A DARKER DAY

The next morning, the Australian trenches resembled a charnel house of dead, wounded and suffering. Those who were able to drag themselves back during the night had to leave behind those slowly dying in no-man's-land, their moans of agony and cries of despair ringing in their ears.

Accompanying Elliott on an inspection of the front line that morning, Lieutenant Jon Schroder described the scene and Pompey's reaction:

Pompey got tired of sitting in advanced brigade headquarters, and took me up the line with him. What had been ordinary sandbagged trenches were now heaps of debris, and it was impossible to walk far without falling over dead men. Although the Hun had a barrage down and there must have been dozens of machine guns operating, Pompey never thought of ducking, but went from battalion to company headquarters and so on right along the line. A word for a wounded man here, a pat of approbation to a bleary-eyed digger there, he missed nobody. He never spoke a word all the way back to advanced brigade head-quarters but went straight inside, put his head in his hands, and sobbed his heart out.

Elliott was a larger than life, famously bombastic character throughout the war and afterwards, but he secretly harboured a depressive nature no doubt intensified by his war experiences. In 1931 he committed suicide. His inability to deal with the con-sequences of the deaths of so many men under his command and particularly those at Fromelles would surely have played a part in his final act of despair. Pompey was loved and revered by his men, and he in turn treasured the lives of each and every one of them. But he could not save them.

All along the Australian front line, the traumatised and bro-ken troops sat in dazed disbelief. The official war correspondent,

Charles Bean, observed, 'The scene in the Australian trenches, packed with wounded and dying, was unexampled in the history of the AIF and was burned into the mind of everyone who saw it.'

The Australians had suffered 5533 casualties. Of those, over 1900 were dead, and many would remain crumpled where they had fallen on the battlefield for the next three years. The infantry of the 5th Australian Division, which had started out with approximately 12 000 soldiers, had effectively ceased to exist.

A comment made later by General Haking can only be described as callous to the point of insulting: 'I think the attack, although it failed, has done both divisions a great deal of good.' The official army communiqué was, to say the least, woefully inadequate: 'Yesterday evening, south of Armentières, we carried out some important raids on a front of two miles in which Australian troops took part. About 140 Germans were captured.'

Chapter 4
WHERE'S MY BOY?

I have a photo of my boy in uniform hanging in my bedroom and often as I look at it the tears roll down my cheeks when thinking what I would give to be able to clasp him in my arms once more.

Agnes 'Nancie' Pearson, fiancée of Robert Courtney Green

For days after the battle, countless individual acts of bravery took place as the survivors attempted to reach the wounded men lying exposed in no-man's-land. Whether it was out of duty, mateship or sheer compassion, their goal was to ease their suffering and, if at all possible, bring the injured back to the relative safety of the trenches.

The would-be rescuers often returned empty-handed, and in some cases they did not return at all. Their sacrifice was compounded by the fact that not only had these men endured the horrors of the battle itself, they were also forced to stay and defend the trenches without a moment's respite, simply because there were not enough reserve troops to replace them.

In a gesture of respect and humanity, the German forces offered a temporary truce to permit the safe passage of the wounded from the battlefield. However, Allied commanders held the haughty view that to accede to a concession of this kind from the enemy was to show weakness and undermine morale, and so, unbelievably, the offer was rejected by headquarters and General McCay.

The general was already extremely unpopular among the Australians. Back in March, McCay had ordered a disastrous training exercise whereby the men of the 14th Brigade were subjected to unnecessary suffering. An unforeseen transport shortage meant the troops had to make their own way from the camp in Tel-el-Kebir to the Suez Canal, 65 kilometres away – a three-day march. Instead of setting off in the late afternoon like the 15th Brigade, they were forced to head across the desert in the heat of the day wearing full battle kit under the blazing Egyptian sun. They didn't have enough water for adequate hydration, and many soldiers became delirious and collapsed on the way. It was a demoralising ordeal.

Four months later, McCay's refusal to allow the temporary truce at Fromelles sealed his reputation, and clearly he never lived it down. His obituary in *The Bulletin* in 1930 described him as 'about the most detested officer in the AIF'.

Thus, it was left to the men in the front lines to risk their own lives saving others. In Hugh Knyvett's book, *Over There with the Australians*, he recalled the astonishing courage of one soldier:

We found a man on the German barbed wire, who was so badly wounded that when we tried to pick him up, one by the shoulders and the other by the feet, it almost seemed that we would pull him apart. The blood was gushing from his mouth, where he had bitten through his lip and tongue, so that he might not jeopardize, by groaning, the chances of some other man who was less badly wounded than he. He begged us to put him out of his misery, but we determined we would get him his chance, though we did not expect him to live. But the sergeant threw himself down on the ground and made of his body a human sledge. Some others joined us and we put the wounded man on his back and dragged them thus across two hundred yards of no-man's-land, through the broken barbed wire and shell-torn ground where every few inches there was a jagged shell, and in and out of shell holes. So anxious were we to get to safety that we did not notice the condition of the man underneath until we got into our trenches; then it was hard to see which was the worst wounded of the two. The sergeant had his hands, face and body torn to ribbons and we had never guessed it, for never once did he ask us to 'slow down' or 'wait a bit'. Such is the stuff that men are made of.

The most famous of these saviours was Sergeant Simon Fraser, the tall and powerful 38-year-old farmer from the Western District of Victoria. Time and again, he ventured out into the bloody wasteland between the lines and staggered back with a wounded comrade. He described in a letter home soon after:

We found a fine haul of wounded and brought them in; but it was not where I heard this fellow calling, so I had another shot for it, and came across a splendid specimen of humanity trying to wriggle into a trench with a big wound in his thigh. He was about 14 stone weight, and I could not lift him on my back; but I managed to get him into an old trench, and told him to lie quiet while I got a stretcher. Then another man about 30 yards out sang out 'Don't forget me, cobber.' I went in and got four volunteers with stretchers, and we got both men in safely.

Fraser is credited with having rescued somewhere in the vicinity of 300 wounded men from no-man's-land. Whether this figure is completely accurate or perhaps tinged with a hint of mythology is irrelevant. What matters is that Fraser, and a score of other saviours, risked their lives, and in some cases gave them, in an extraordinary bid to rescue a great many of their comrades.

Fraser survived the battle and was later promoted to the rank of 2nd Lieutenant, but he was killed the following year at Bullecourt. Sadly, he was not plucked from the battlefield as he had done for so many others, and to this day his body has never been recovered. It is a fitting tribute, therefore, that the Cobbers statue prominently displayed at both the Australian Memorial Park outside Fromelles and the Shrine of Remembrance in Melbourne is an evocative depiction of Fraser with a wounded comrade flung over his back as he carries him to safety.

So what became of the dead?

The vast majority of Australians who fell in the battle did so either in no-man's-land or behind the German lines. Of those who died in the Australian trenches or succumbed to their wounds later on, most were identified and buried in battlefield cemeteries created behind the front lines. Today, the headstones that mark the graves of these men can be found in a number of Commonwealth War Graves Commission cemeteries located in the surrounding area, including Rue-Petillon, Rue du Bois and Ration Farm.

For those who died in no-man's-land, the story is very different. Although there were men willing to risk their lives to recover the wounded, there was far less motivation to do so for those beyond help. What's more, the battlefield at Fromelles had the dubious distinction of staying almost entirely static throughout the war. Even taking into account the stagnant nature of trench warfare on the Western Front, in the two and a half years following the battle until the conclusion of hostilities, the front lines moved back and forth practically everywhere except at Fromelles.

Flanked on both sides by the two foremost British spheres of action, the Somme to the south and Ypres to the north, the opposing armies largely maintained a defensive position within the existing trenches around Fromelles. Consequently, the ground between the front lines remained unoccupied by either side and could not be cleared of the dead until after the signing of the armistice on 11 November 1918.

Upon that momentous occasion, war correspondent Charles

Bean chose to go immediately to Fromelles before visiting any other field of battle where Australians had fought. In his diary, he described the scene:

> *We found the old No-man's land simply full of our dead. In the narrow sector west of the Laies river and east of the corner of the sugarloaf salient the skulls and bones and torn uniforms were lying about everywhere. I found a bit of Australian kit lying 50 yards from the corner of the salient; and the bones of an Australian officer and several men within 100 yards of it.*

The ravages of time and of the elements, as well as the effects of constant warfare in the area, had taken their toll. Men who were once considered among the finest Australia could offer had been reduced to torn rags, strewn kit and bleached bones. These remains were eventually collected from the battlefield after the ceasefire by the Graves Services Unit and buried in the newly constructed VC Corner Military Cemetery nearby.

In all, 410 men were recovered and yet not one of them could be identified. Consequently, they were interred in forty-one groups of ten and, unlike the majority of Commonwealth cemeteries, there were no individual headstones. Instead, two sizeable stone crosses were set into the lawn surrounded by rosebushes, each plant signifying a soldier lying beneath. It is the only all-Australian cemetery in France and lies at the heart of the former battlefield.

The stone memorial wall constructed by the Imperial War Graves Commission at the rear of the cemetery records the names of the 1299 Australians missing from the battle, inscribed on panels across its breadth. Decades later, this list of names became the catalyst that triggered the search for the missing dead of Fromelles.

Immediately after the battle, signs of the desperate fight for survival in and beyond the German front lines were plain for all to see. Smashed parapets, destroyed dugouts, wrecked equipment and the general debris of war littered the countryside.

A major preoccupation for those German soldiers holding the line was to consolidate and rebuild their defensive works in the event of a renewed Allied attack. No doubt of equal importance was to clear the trenches of the dead and wounded. Health and morale depended on it.

Major General Julius Ritter von Braun, who was in command of the troops opposing the Australians, ordered the excavation of mass graves for up to 400 English soldiers behind Pheasant Wood:

> *The English bodies will be buried in mass graves immediately to the south of Pheasant Wood . . . In order to expedite the rapid removal of the bodies, the dead are to be separated by nationality and laid at depots close to the light railway . . . For the burial of the English dead, H-Company is to excavate mass graves for approximately 400 bodies.*

This site lay approximately 200 metres north of Fromelles itself. Allied aerial photographs taken in the days after the battle show that the graves were most likely dug on or about 22 July. The selection of Pheasant Wood by von Braun was almost certainly influenced by the fact that the Germans had previously constructed a light railway leading from their front lines to the rear, cutting through the south-west corner of the wood en route.

Eight pits, excavated to a size approximately 10 metres in length and 2 metres in width, were prepared in two rows of four on the south side of Pheasant Wood. It was to this location that the bodies, most of them Australian, were transported on the flatbed wagons of the railway. Bloody khaki-clad corpses piled two or three high rumbled to the pit-side. Some were already wrapped in groundsheets, others bound with wire or bandages, but many remained just as they had been found, in the anguished poses of death.

Before they were buried, the Germans stripped the bodies of almost all identification, including their discs and pay books. Items of a more personal nature, such as diaries, letters, bibles and coins, were also removed:

> *The removal of effects and identity discs . . . is to be carried out by H-Company, supported by one medical NCO and four men of the regiment; under the orders of the Regimental Medical Officer . . . and will collect papers and identity discs in such a way that the personal effects and identity disc are removed from each body individually and are immediately placed in a sandbag, tied off and tagged with a cardboard or stiff paper label on which the number and company appearing on the identity disc are recorded.*

Although souveniring personal belongings was a reasonably common occurrence throughout the Great War and no doubt took place at Fromelles, much of what was removed from the Australian dead prior to their burial at Pheasant Wood eventually found its way back to grieving relatives. For this, the families have the astute Bavarian commander von Braun to thank: 'The misappropriation of even the most insignificant item of property from a body (German or English) constitutes robbery of the dead and will be severely punished.'

When all the personal items had been removed, it was time to fill the pits. Each one was packed with a layer of bodies, a sprinkling of lime, and then a shallow deposit of soil before a second tier of bodies was placed on top. As each pit reached capacity, it was backfilled and covered over with the excavated earth.

At first, the Germans performed their job carefully and laid the remains in neat rows, head to tail along the length of each pit. But, as the day wore on, the sight and stench of blood-soaked uniforms, missing limbs and gaping wounds would have taken their toll, and the best intentions of the burial party gave way to expediency. The placement of each body became more haphazard, until all care was abandoned and the last ones were unceremoniously tossed one on top of the other.

The Germans allowed for up to 400 sets of remains to be buried at this site, but they eventually interred 250. As a consequence, only five of the pits were filled. The remaining three were left largely empty and stayed open until at least September 1918.

Bill Barry was a plumber and gasfitter from Northcote in Melbourne who kept an extraordinary 65 000-word diary of his war experiences. Apart from its general historical value, it contains the strong suggestion that Bill actually witnessed the Pheasant Wood burial. A private with the 29th Battalion, Barry had been knocked unconscious by a shell during the battle and, when he came around the following morning, discovered that he was quite badly wounded in the leg and a prisoner of war. After being robbed and soundly beaten on a number of occasions the next day, he ended up at a German Red Cross post further behind the lines. As he describes it:

> *To my horror, I was in the place where all the dead men were. I was sitting on the edge of a hole about forty feet long, twenty feet wide and fifteen feet deep and into this hole the dead were being thrown without any fuss or respect. It was pitiful to see the different expressions on their faces, some with a peaceful smile and others showed they had passed away in agony.*

Due to the severe nature of his wounds, Barry was sent to a German hospital. The doctors there treated him well, although they had to amputate his leg. He was eventually repatriated to England just before the war ended and, after taking tea at Windsor Castle with Princess Beatrice, he returned home safely to Northcote.

Once the disposal of the bodies was complete, it was time to notify the families and pass on any details of their loved ones' final resting places. On the surface, this would appear to be a simple task, but the circumstances of war and protracted communication trails led to what we now know was a tremendous amount of confusion and misinterpretation that went on for many years.

Soon after the battle, each unit conducted a roll call to determine who was missing. This was when the survivors had a chance to tell what they knew about those unaccounted for. Unit records were then updated accordingly and AIF Headquarters in London was advised. The information was forwarded to Base Records in Melbourne and then finally sent to families via telegram.

Bob Green's fiancée, Nancie, had just seen his name in the list of 'Missing' from the Western Australia newspaper casualty lists when she wrote to Bob's mother in England in a letter dated 25 September 1916:

> I was nearly demented when I saw the dear boy's name in the paper . . . Since then I have heard nothing from him whatever and I am nearly mad with grief. This blow is almost more than I can bear. I loved him more than words can tell and to think that perhaps he may be gone from me forever is to [sic] dreadful.

Instead of saying that their soldier was simply 'missing', there were times when telegrams offered a glimmer of hope. Families were told that their man was 'missing, believed prisoner of war' on the basis of statements made by other soldiers. These generally uncorroborated comments from the soldier's comrades might be as simple as someone reporting that they'd seen the soldier lying wounded in the German lines when the Australians retreated so there was a chance he was a prisoner of war. Although there was necessarily a great deal of guesswork at that time, it seems somewhat unsympathetic to knowingly convey this (usually false) hope to relatives without first confirming or at least reasonably substantiating the evidence.

In one extreme example, a particular 'witness' told of an encounter he had in London some months after the battle with a soldier who had been reported missing. The soldier in question was posted as absent without leave and later listed as a deserter. The stain on his file and the consequent humiliation of his family were removed only recently when documentation confirmed he had been killed in action at Fromelles.

For Nancie, the hope that Bob was still alive was kindled by ambiguous information from the authorities:

> Perhaps they can't find the dear boys remains, that is why he is reported missing and there is just the slight hope that he may be a prisoner of war.
>
> I have been making all sorts of enquiries to see if I can find out anything. First I went to the Department of Defence here and now I have got the Red Cross trying to find him for me, and as you can imagine, I am anxiously awaiting the results of their investigation.

Late in 1916 lists began arriving at Allied headquarters via the Red Cross in Switzerland. These were the *Nachlassliste*, or death lists, prepared by the Germans from the identification discs and other property removed from the dead and then forwarded on to the Red Cross. Although they clearly spelled out the names of those Allied soldiers who had been killed, there was still an element of confusion as the lists were misinterpreted to be the names of men who had died as prisoners of war. This is evident in another letter Nancie sent to Bob's mother some months later:

> *I had a letter from the Red Cross to say that Bob had been posted in the German death lists on the 4th of November as having died of wounds while a prisoner of war. Now I have just had another report to say that they were wrong. In the above statement, they find now that our dear one had never been a prisoner of war at all but that he died on the battlefield and his identification disc had been taken from his body by the Germans before they buried him.*

The only decisive answer they ever received was a package sent from Germany via the Red Cross in Switzerland, containing his bloodstained identity disc.

Of course, many families who received messages that their relatives had died as prisoners of war understandably assumed there would be a corresponding grave. It seemed suspicious to them when no such grave was ever reported, and many relatives believed the original notification was in fact an error and that their man must still be alive and imprisoned somewhere by the Germans.

Heinrich 'Theo' Pflaum and his brother Friedrich 'Fritz' migrated to Australia from Holstein, Germany, in the late 1860s and made their home in Blumberg, South Australia. The two men soon gained prominence in their new society, and both became highly respected business and community leaders in their own right.

Raising his family of Australian-born children, Theo could not have shown more patriotic love for his adopted country than if he had been born there himself. When his three sons enlisted with the AIF at the outbreak of war, no father could have been prouder. The youngest of Theo's three sons, Ray, was with his battalion on the evening of 19 July 1916 and hopped the bags at Fromelles. He was mortally wounded by shrapnel in the stomach, and his compatriots had to leave him to die in the German trenches. Ray's older brother, Theo Jr (whose exploits crossing no-man's-land were recounted earlier), described his final meeting with Ray only moments after gaining the relative safety of the German front line:

> While the men were getting their wind my attention was drawn to a wounded man alongside me just along a dugout. It was Ray. I ran down to him and was told he had a piece of shrapnel in the stomach just as he was able to get into their trench. He was quite conscious and by his appearance he didn't seem to be hit too badly. One of the 32nd fellers helped me put him into the dugout. I spoke to him and told him that our fellers had taken their third line so it was certain we would be able to hold the first. I managed to get him a flask of whiskey and a mouthful

of that seemed to make his spirits go up. He was not in a great deal of pain whilst lying still but he could not bear to be moved. Although this takes time to write, it was all done in a minute or so. There were dozens of wounded about but I asked a 32nd feller, slightly wounded in the foot, to do the best for Ray while he could. I then made my way down to find a position for my gun.

It wasn't until November 1916 that the Australian Headquarters in London received a German death list dated 3 November, naming Raymond Pflaum as one of the Australian soldiers killed at Fromelles on 19 July. Without any clear reason, Headquarters decided that Ray had officially died on 24 November as a prisoner of war. This was in fact the date they received the list and it is now evident that a serious administration bungle had been made. None of the staff picked up that the date was not only patently incorrect but they were also pronouncing Pflaum's death as being three weeks after the death list itself was compiled.

In 1917 a confused Theo Pflaum wrote of his dilemma in a letter to Base Records:

On July 20th last year my son fell in the charge at Fleurbaix [Fromelles]. According to information received he was in the front line of the attack and was mortally wounded by a shell wound to the stomach. And as informed by returned invalided comrades of his, he bled profusely and could not possibly live many hours. They pulled him in to a little dugout and placed him as comfortably as possible. My other son who was in the

same engagement in the Machine Gun section happened by
chance to come across him a little later, who still found him
conscious, calm and resigned 'though weak' . . . On Dec 18th/16
cable was received from Red Cross Commissioners, London,
informing us that the name of the above soldier appears in
the German Death List. Official information was sent to my
wife . . . that the above had died whilst a prisoner of war.
On Feb 1st the Major from Keswick Barracks writes that the
death of the above had not yet been officially confirmed by
the German authorities . . . When such was not sent on in the
last seven months and definite information of his death only
obtained when finally the Red Cross researchers dug it up out of
the German Death List and with all other private information,
we have had the assurance of his death 'as not long after he fell'
for months past . . .

In the face of irrefutable evidence discovered at the German
Imperial War Office after the war, Base Records still clung to
the snippet of cabled information it had received in 1916 and
reiterated that Ray had died in November, either disregarding
or misunderstanding the newly found German documentation.
In a letter replying to an enquiry from Ray's sister in 1921, the
officer in charge at Base Records wrote, 'and in reply to state
the only information available from German records is to the
effect that the above named soldier fell in the neighbourhood of
Fromelles on 19/7/16 and died in Germany on 24/11/16'.

Because his official date of death as a prisoner of war was
recorded months after the Fromelles engagement, Ray's name

had been omitted from the VC Corner Memorial, where it rightfully belonged alongside the names of the comrades with whom he had fought. And later, when an unknown employee at Base Records recognised the glaring oversight and attempted to correct it by adding a note to Ray's service record, it wasn't for another ninety-five years that the date was officially amended.

Theo Pflaum willingly offered three sons to his adopted country and endured the loss of two, who paid the supreme sacrifice, yet he and his family were forced to suffer the indignities of anti-German sentiment throughout the war. Fritz served faithfully in the South Australian House of Assembly for many years, and then, by an act of Parliament, he was deemed to be unacceptable as a member because of his German ancestry. When the Geographical Names Board was charged with the job of anglicising names of German origin, they made an unsuccessful bid to alter the name of Pflaum Street, Blumberg, to something more 'appropriate'. However, they did successfully change the name of Theo's beloved town to Birdwood. In 1920 Theo invited General Sir William Birdwood to visit the town named in his honour. Birdwood seemed quite impressed with his host and paid warm tribute to Theo after his death:

He once told me 'I was born a Dane. Germany and Austria attacked and split up my country and I became Austrian. Germany attacked and defeated Austria and I became a German. When old enough, my brother and I were called up to enlist in the Prussian army. We said nothing doing, and at once came to Australia where we have been very happy and never regretted our freedom here.'

Theo Pflaum never learned what happened to his son.

Chapter 5

IN WHOM WE TRUST

Up to present we cannot get a satisfactory statement from the Graves Registration Unit or Directorate of Graves Registration regarding the removal of collective graves before Pheasant Wood.

Major Alfred Allen, Australian Graves Services, February 1920

It wasn't until 1917, when next of kin began receiving identity discs and personal property from Germany, that people started to accept the soldiers were gone. Most of the relatives now understood that there was no chance they'd survived. But, for some, the doubt lingered on even when the German Imperial War Records were examined after the war and documents that confirmed the deaths were released:

Intelligence Officer,
At Chief Army Command
To the Imperial Prussian War Office, Medical Section,
Central Office for Left Property, Berlin.

The Australian soldier (name) fell on 19/7/16 in the neighbour-
hood of Fromelles.
Captain & Intelligence Officer
Undersigned
Attested, Berlin 1/10/19
(Signed) Jacobi
Lt. Of Res.

The cynical mistrust of all official reports resulting from the original notification debacle was still very much in evidence. Without a grave, without a body, without an explanation, some relatives still clung desperately to false hopes. For these people, the war never ended.

Confusion surrounding the fate and whereabouts of Private Allan Irving is painfully clear in his service file held by the National Archives of Australia. A bookbinder from South Australia, he was still serving with the Citizen Military Forces when he enlisted with the 32nd Battalion in July 1915. As he was reported missing after the battle, his mother, Alice, waited for more decisive intelligence about her son, but instead she was subject to the full gamut of emotions at each conflicting report. Exasperated, she finally wrote to Base Records to help her make sense of what had happened: 'Missing since July 20th, 1916, reported by Red Cross on the death list of Nov 4th 1916 in Germany, later reported unofficially prisoner of war in Germany (Feb 16th 1917). Please give further information if possible . . .'

First she was told her son was missing, then she was advised that his name appeared on a German death list, and then she was notified that he was unofficially recorded as a prisoner of war. The response she received from the above letter informed her (incorrectly) that he had died as a prisoner of war. In the end, she learned and came to accept that her precious son had died on the field of battle at Fromelles. The tortuous emotional journey she had experienced to that point would have only intensified her grief.

Misinformation was rife. A number of men from the 31st Battalion were officially recorded as missing on 21 July 1916, the day after the battle. This was the date that was nominally provided by battalion headquarters because it was the day they called the roll and discovered the men unaccounted for. They were not to know that the consequences of this decision were far-reaching, for the deaths of these men fell outside the official dates of the battle. As a result, their names were omitted from the VC Corner Memorial and added instead to the Villers-Bretonneux Memorial over 80 kilometres south of Fromelles, on the Somme River.

For the majority of relatives, dealing with the Base Records Office was a deeply frustrating process. Constantly inundated with correspondence and enquiries, the office quickly became overwhelmed. Information from overseas was agonisingly slow and the news that did eventually arrive was often just ill-informed notifications to be passed on to families. To some extent, the Australian Red Cross Wounded and Missing Enquiry Bureau managed to fill this void and offer families another source of investigation. It was headed by the irrepressible Vera Deakin, who was the daughter of a future Australian

prime minister. Deakin offered her services to the Australian
Red Cross early in the war and, the day after joining them in
Cairo in 1915, she opened the first bureau office devoted to ·
finding information for relatives of Australian soldiers who were
serving on Gallipoli. Shifting operations to London when the
AIF transferred to the Western Front, the bureau expanded
and employed agents in England, France and Belgium to interview soldiers, comb through official casualty lists and liaise with
other agencies. When a death was reported, the Red Cross staff
did everything in their power to eliminate doubt.

In many cases, the letters back to families quoted eyewitness
statements directly from the mouths of soldiers, who were often
brutally explicit in detail. But with so many relatives desperate
for any news they could get, the Australian Red Cross resolutely
supplied every piece of information they came across no matter
how graphic, and the Australian public was grateful. To know
the horrifying facts was preferable to knowing nothing at all.

By the end of the war, the bureau had grown to over sixty
staff, had handled approximately 32 000 individual cases and
responded to enquiries in more than 400 000 letters. Vera
Deakin's determination and advocacy convinced families that
the Australian Red Cross was a faster and more thorough alternative to the formal responses offered by the army.

Nevertheless, even the Australian Red Cross Wounded and
Missing Enquiry Bureau didn't always get their facts right.
Reports from various soldiers could be wildly contradictory or
just plain wrong, and on occasion the meaning of an official
report would be misconstrued and passed on.

The last sighting of Private Clifford Holliday of the 54th Battalion was in the front German trench. He had been shot in the face and was sitting near the entrance to the communication trench. A number of his comrades saw him there before the retreat and, although they knew such a wound was incapacitating, not one of them thought it would be mortal. In early August 1916, the Reverend Andrew Holliday, of Hornsby, Sydney, was informed that his son had been wounded. Expecting further updates regarding his condition and which hospital he had been admitted to, Holliday waited anxiously. After a week with no further news, Holliday wrote to Base Records and asked them to make more enquiries. He also explained that he had engaged the services of the Red Cross. Following a further series of cables back and forth to London, no more information was forthcoming except to say that Clifford was wounded. By September, Holliday was frantic about the welfare of his son and wrote a barrage of letters to Base Records, local members of Parliament and anyone else who might be able to assist. In a reply to him on 4 September, Base Records again explained that there was nothing more to tell other than 'wounded 19th or 20th July', but for some reason added, 'From this it can only be assumed that your son is making satisfactory progress, as had he developed dangerous or serious symptoms, the authorities of the hospital in which he was located would have telegraphed immediately.'

It's no surprise that, on 6 December, Holliday refused to accept the content of the cable that arrived announcing his son's death. His mistrust of official reports increased even further when he saw that the date supplied for Clifford's death was 30 July. In response to his immediate query, a second cable was sent to him the following day amending it to the 20th. But the damage had been done, and he wrote back:

> *Had we been told on 9th August that our boy had been killed in action we would have accepted it, for we had counted the cost. But to tell it to us now in this mistaken and mixed up fashion simply staggers us. It baffles words to tell what agonized heart-ache such mistakes have caused us.*

Meanwhile, the Red Cross Wounded and Missing Enquiry Bureau had interviewed a number of soldiers who had seen Clifford wounded, but none of their statements indicated he was likely to have died. In fact, they were quite to the contrary, supporting the original report that he was only wounded. While the army attempted to convince Holliday that the report of Clifford's death was accurately obtained from a German death list stating he fell in the neighbourhood of Fromelles, the Red Cross put a slightly different spin on the information. In a letter written to Holliday, they explained:

> *This may, we fear, possibly mean that your son has fallen and that he has been found by the burying party and the Pay Book taken from the body. In the absence of particulars we cannot however accept this as an absolute certainty. Cases have come to our notice at times when the notice has appeared and then the owner of the disc has eventually turned up alive.*

Under the circumstances, the distraught Reverend Holliday was only too willing to grasp any shred of hope, continuing to correspond and request answers from the authorities for several years. It was not until 1923 that a captain at Base Records finally put the pieces together:

> *It is abundantly clear that the Australian Forces were heavily engaged in the action at Fromelles on 19/7/16 and were unable to properly facilitate the withdrawal of the wounded owing to their enforced retirement. The ultimate fate of those left on the battlefield was thus to a very large extent determined by the evidence of individual witnesses . . . In the case of your son a report was received . . . indicating that he fell in the vicinity of Fromelles, and was identified by means of a disc and pay book found on his person.*

There was also a revealing document located in Clifford Holliday's service file in the form of a letter written from Base Records to his father in August 1923. In addition to confirming his death, it hinted at the kind of actions that had been taken to locate graves in the Fromelles area and the presumption that arose as a result of that search:

> *You are advised that the regimental particulars of Private C. D. Holliday are shown in lists which have been received from Berlin, relative to a burial by the Germans, in one of several graves in Fromelles. Extensive searches have been made with a view to locating these graves but without success and*

it is thought that these graves have been found in the course
of exhumation and the bodies re-buried as 'Unknowns' in the
concentration cemeteries for the area.

From this, we can deduce that the search for battlefield graves
in the Fromelles area had ceased by this date. The authorities
had reached agreement that the remains were part of the general
exhumations collected from the surrounding area and reburied
together as 'Known Unto God' in one of the newly constructed
Imperial War Graves Commission cemeteries. But what information about the mass graves was known, who undertook the
search, and exactly how 'extensive' was it?

The first official mention that we have of the mass graves
at Pheasant Wood comes from Major General Julius Ritter von
Braun, who ordered the pits to be prepared the day after the
battle. On that same date, they were also mentioned in the 21st
Bavarian Reserve Infantry Regiment War Diary. As these documents were not available to the Allies, the question remains
when, or indeed if, the Allies were ever notified.

The answer to this can be found in the files of two
Australian officers: 2nd Lieutenant John 'Jack' Bowden of
the 59th Battalion and Lieutenant Robert Burns of the 14th
Machine Gun Company. A 35-year-old bank manager from
South Yarra, Melbourne, Jack Bowden enlisted as a private
with the 31st Battalion, was transferred to the 59th soon after
arriving in Egypt and was almost immediately promoted to
the rank of 2nd lieutenant. Apparently, he was cut down relatively early in the battle at Fromelles. Accurate details about his

fate are difficult to establish but what can be ascertained from the files is that his remains were recovered by the Germans and buried.

His sister was notified of his death in August 1916 via a German death list, and the subsequent requests she made to the Australian Red Cross regarding the whereabouts of his property and confusion about his being a prisoner of war prompted an enquiry with the Central Committee of the German Red Cross Societies. The response she received in January 1918 represents the first-known notification given to the Allies of the existence of the graves at Pheasant Wood:

> *After the battle near Fromelles on the 19.7.16 the identity discs were removed from all the fallen men and sent in. The name of Bowden is not reported in the lists of graves. It may be assumed that possibly Lieutenant Bowden was buried in one of the five large British collective graves before the Fasanen Waldchen (Pheasants Wood) near Fromelles, or in the collective grave (No.1 M.4.3) in the Military Cemetery at Fournes.*

Little more is made of this information in Bowden's file except that, in 1920, it was decided his grave was actually at Fournes. But this assumption was soon proved to be wrong when the exhumation at Fournes that followed did not uncover his remains. How exactly this 'fact' was determined is not evident in his file, but an examination of documents relating to Lieutenant Robert Burns provides an insight into what occurred.

Housed in the National Archives of Australia is a file titled
'Court of Inquiry – to Inquire into and Report upon certain
matters in connection with the Australian Graves Services'. The
Court of Inquiry was convened in 1920 for the express purpose
of investigating not only allegations of gross misconduct but
also claims that representatives of the Burns family were misled
by both the head of the Australian Graves Services, Major G. L.
Phillips, and its inspector in France, Major Alfred Allen. These
men were suspected of deliberately deceiving the Burnses and
subjecting them to a hoax regarding the burial of their son.

Sir James Burns, founder of Burns, Philp & Co. Limited,
was a businessman, shipowner, philanthropist and close friend
to the governor general of Australia. He was devastated by
the loss of his son and desperately wanted to recover Robert's
remains. He communicated with the Australian authorities in
London, and then sent a representative from his company's
London office to make follow-up enquiries.

Under pressure to locate the grave of Burns' son, in early
1920 the Australian Graves Services announced that they
believed they had found Robert in the Military Cemetery at
Fournes. Immediately, Burns' representative, Mr C. A. Smith,
requested he be present at the exhumation. Although he was
initially denied permission by Phillips, the decision was over-
turned when representations were made to higher authorities.
Smith then claimed that, although it was promised that he
would be given several days' warning prior to exhuming the
site, Phillips had instead written to Allen with instructions to
exhume any bodies at Fournes before Smith could arrive:

*For God's sake have it carried out immediately if at all possible,
and then advise me that the exhumation has been completed.
This may not be possible, but you understand the position, and
you can quite see that I do not wish to suffer any loss of dignity
when it refers to a man whose principles are certainly rather
doubtful.*

Suspecting a deception, and concerned that a deliberately false
identification might be made simply to satisfy the continual
requests of the Burns family, Smith decided to travel to France of
his own volition and took everyone by surprise when he arrived
the day before the scheduled exhumation. Smith then witnessed
what he described as deliberate delays and cover-ups, until finally
he was present for the exhumation, during which no remains of
Robert Burns or indeed of any Australians were found. It must
be said that Allen denied ever receiving Phillips' letter, and certainly his subsequent actions do not reflect a person who was
attempting to expedite the exhumation at Phillips' behest.

Whether or not there is any truth to the allegations made by
Smith and the Burns family, the Court of Inquiry records tell us
much about what the authorities knew of the Pheasant Wood
graves and the efforts made to locate them. In his statement to
the court, Major Phillips recalled:

*The records in Australia House show that a letter dated 12th
day of March, 1919, was received from the Officer in Charge
of Records, Administrative Headquarters, AIF, London*

addressed to the Corps Burial Officer of the Australian Graves Registration Section France and relative to Lieutenant R. D. Burns . . . It was also stated that a communication was received from Germany giving the information that there were five large collective British Graves before Pheasants Wood and also a German Military Cemetery at Fournes. It was asked that a search be made. A digest of these facts was forwarded to Major Allen, then Inspector of the AIF Graves Section in France.

Following Phillips' testimony, Major Allen was called as a witness to the events. In his affidavit to the court, he briefly explained what action he eventually took in early 1920, some months after he received the request from Phillips in September:

I made an exhaustive search all round Fromelles, Pheasant Wood and a portion of Fournes. I traced where a cross had been removed but no one knew where, and after a further search I located this cross in Fournes Cemetery, the only cross of its kind with the date of death and the word 'Fromelles' on the cross.

The details of his search in the reports he prepared at the time were tendered to the court as evidence. These provide us with the only specific material regarding the hunt for the Pheasant Wood graves in the years after the war:

I carried out a personal search, walking many miles in various areas, trying to locate the reported isolated collective grave supposed to hold Lieut. Burns and others. Near Fromelles a

place was pointed as where the Germans exhumed English sol-
diers. A little cemetery on the other side of Fromelles was found
and from this bodies had been removed. After further search,
the original cross, as was reported at Fromelles was located in
Fournes Military Cemetery. The inscription and date thereon
exactly corresponded with the cross as reported by Headquarters,
London as being described by the Germans.

. . . the cross referred to in my former letter as being in a
German Cemetery at Fournes is in my opinion the cross and
grave asked for, as the cross and grave were originally placed by
the Germans at a spot near Fromelles and Pheasant Wood and
since collected by them and replaced in this cemetery.

But perhaps the most telling document was the results of the exhumation in the unsuccessful hunt for Lieutenants Bowden and Burns at Fournes. This indicated that the original reports referring to the graves of both men at Pheasant Wood had been negated by Allen's belief that the bodies had been moved to Fournes.

From Allen's description of his search, the clear inference is that he was shown to the site of the Pheasant Wood graves and very likely stood on the ground where the remains still lay beneath his feet. Owing to what seems like nothing more than anecdotal evidence, he formed the opinion that the bodies and cross that marked their resting place had been moved to Fournes. The fact that all available documentary evidence unmistakably identified both sites as coexisting independently appears to have been missed or ignored by Allen, and it seems that it never occurred to him that there might have been two crosses.

After the war, Alfred Allen had come to the Australian Graves Services from the Red Cross, and the nominal rank of major was bestowed upon him for the task ahead. Credited with having recovered a great many missing Australian remains from battlefield graves, he was generally regarded as highly skilled. In an article written about him in 1924 by John Oxenham, Allen was lauded as:

A born leader of men, with a most remarkable memory, an intuitive perception of possibilities, and a mind trained to minute observation and deduction . . . Are there any indications of bodies still below? His trained sense leads him here, there. It may be a patch of more luxuriant growth in the herbage; it may be – other things. He carries with him a specially made slender steel rod with an oblong slot in its sharp point, and with it he delicately probes the soil in all likely spots . . . And in a manner little short of magical the earth yields up its secrets to him.

But, given the allegations of the Burns family, together with explosive claims – some wildly outlandish, others probable fact – of drunkenness, running prostitution rings, corruption, nepotism, mal-administration and desecration within the ranks of the Australian War Graves Service in France at the time of the Pheasant Wood search, it's no wonder that the Court of Inquiry recorded:

Opportunity for abuse is great and unless the most rigid control and discipline is maintained this work intended to sanctify and hallow the memory of the dead must develop into a serious scandal bringing humiliation and disgrace upon the Australian Forces. Up to the date of investigation by this Court of Inquiry, no reasonable or definite plan of carrying out the work seems to have been formed and many of the officers and men selected did not realize the dignity and importance of their position. The appalling condition apparent in March 1920 must come as a warning for the future guidance of those in charge, that unless immediate and drastic action is taken for proper control, this effort to honour the dead shall only be the means of bringing shame and disgrace upon the good name, fame and reputation of Australia.

However noble a task, we must take into account the reality that digging up the rotting corpses of long-dead former comrades would have been an appalling job. Without superhuman levels of moral fortitude to cope with what they had to do, the men of the Australian Graves Services in France may well have found alternative ways to pass the time during their private moments to help them cope with what they had seen. They may also have been less than diligent when faced with the choice of having to dig through another mass grave or just leave it alone.

Either way, it seems that in the hunt for the Pheasant Wood graves, Allen's intuitive perception and powers of deduction were not at their best. We can only conclude that perhaps the search wasn't quite as comprehensive as he would have liked us to believe.

Chapter 6

DETERMINED
ADVOCATES

It almost seems to me now that no one knows and no one even cares
what has become of my son.

Reverend Andrew Holliday, father of Clifford Dawson Holliday

It's difficult for some people to associate a Greek-born art
teacher with an Anzac tradition that has long been bred into
those of us who have a direct personal family attachment. But
in Lambis Englezos, we see that it is not necessary to have an
ancestral history of representing Australia in times of conflict
to embrace the Anzac values of endurance, courage, ingenuity
and mateship. You merely need to accept yourself as Australian
and allow Dorethea Mackellar's vision of 'a sunburnt country'
to enter your heart and mind.

Born in Salonika in the early 1950s, Lambis was only one
year old when he joined the thousands of 'new Australians'
migrating to Australia. His father, Evangelos, was a farmer

in northern Greece and served with the Greek Army fighting the Germans during the Second World War. After the war, he became disenchanted with his homeland as a result of the ongoing political strife and brutal civil war between the Western-backed government forces and communist-supported democratic army. Determined to provide better opportunities for his wife and new child, in 1954 Evangelos took advantage of the Australian migrant initiative to boost population. Leaving Greece, he set out with his family to begin life anew in Australia.

Along with thousands of migrants entering Australia in the 1950s, the Englezos family were housed in the rudimentary accommodation blocks at Bonegilla Migrant Camp in northeast Victoria. Bonegilla was a staging camp for new arrivals who had exchanged free or assisted passage to Australia for two years of labour. Once this agreement was honoured, migrants were entitled to make their own way.

When finally free of his obligations, Evangelos moved his family from the remote Bonegilla area to Melbourne, where they settled in the largest Greek community outside Greece. His new home was located in a leafy bayside suburb of the Victorian capital city, and young Lambis took to his surroundings and adopted country like a duck to the local Albert Park Lake.

For many Australian children of the era, primary school was their introduction to the Anzac Day ceremony and its heritage. Lambis was captivated by its symbolism and began keeping company with old diggers from the neighbourhood, listening to their tales of the war, soaking it all up like a sponge. He maintained his interest in the Great War throughout his formative years.

Eventually Lambis became a high-school arts and crafts teacher. While advancing his career and providing for his own growing family, he continued to read voraciously about Australia's involvement in the Great War. It was some time before he came across a reference to a little French village called Fromelles and the tragedy that unfolded in the fields nearby. Amazed at the distinct lack of public awareness about one of the most tragic events in Australian history, he took it upon himself to discover more. He had no idea what he was getting into.

The friendships he had formed with old soldiers in the area and his passion for understanding the events of the Great War brought him into contact with a great many like-minded people. It was through these associations that he came to assist in the formation of the 'Friends of the 15th Brigade'. The soldiers of the 15th had fought at both Gallipoli and on the Western Front, and it was through the family, friends and the few elderly surviving members of the brigade that Lambis first heard eyewitness accounts of Fromelles and its aftermath.

Men such as Tom Brain of the 60th Battalion, Bill Boyce of the 58th and Fred Kelly of the 53rd became his firm friends. They told him of the confusion, chaos and horror of Fromelles. He was deeply moved by the raw expressions of emotion from these active participants and was able to picture in his mind the hellish microcosm that was their war. But the picture could never be complete for Lambis until he was actually able to tread the roads and fields that he could only visualise. And so, in 1996, on the occasion of the 80th anniversary of the Fromelles battle, he made a pilgrimage to the tiny northern French town.

Immersing himself in the surroundings, he explored the battle-field, visited the cemeteries and envisaged the scene through the eyes of the veterans whose stories he had come to know so well. If Lambis thought that just one visit would satisfy his curiosity about the place, he was very much mistaken. For it was to be the first of many visits, and now this little piece of France has almost become his second home.

His next visit to Fromelles, in 2002, marked the beginning of the search for Pheasant Wood. Accompanying him on his many wanders around the area was Fromelles local Martial Delebarre, whose family have lived there for several centuries. Martial happened to be the Commonwealth War Graves representative for the area and was one of the founders of the local L'Association pour le Souvenir de la Bataille de Fromelles. He also helped to create an outstanding little museum commemorating the battle inside the Fromelles Town Hall. (It's no surprise that Martial was subsequently awarded the Order of Australia.) Lambis could not have had a more knowledgeable and inspirational companion, passing on an endless stream of facts and stories as they trod the fields together.

When Lambis revisited VC Corner Cemetery, he felt once again the overwhelming sadness of the place. This time, however, he experienced a growing sense of unease about the names and the numbers before him, and he took out his notepad and pencil. In his first amateurish attempts to add up the figures, he realised there was a significant discrepancy between the list of Australians killed during the battle and buried at VC Corner and surrounding cemeteries and the list of men still missing. He knew that there would have been a small number virtually vaporised by shellfire, but there's no way this would have accounted for the figure of 250 that his calculations had arrived at. So where were they?

When he arrived back in Australia, Lambis began publicly posing his questions among members of the Great War historical community, attracting a small band of amateur historians with an interest in Fromelles. The first to join the quest alongside Lambis were John Fielding, Ward Selby and Robin Corfield, foremost expert on Fromelles and author of the definitive book about the battle itself, called *Don't Forget Me, Cobber*.

The first concrete piece of evidence to back up Lambis's idea came from the pages of Robin's book. It contained a portion of the chronicle of Private Bill Barry, the Australian soldier captured during the battle who woke up to the sight of dead soldiers being buried in a mass grave. Lambis hypothesised that this may be the answer to the missing men, but Barry's account gave scant detail and no hints as to where the grave might be. It was a start but by no means definitive proof.

Applying their combined knowledge, the group explored the theory of a mass grave somewhere along the route of the German light-railway system. With ample evidence in both historical records and photographs of light railways being used to transport the dead on flatbed wagons away from their trenches, it was reasonable to suggest that the Germans had acted similarly at Fromelles. Examining the light-railway system behind the German lines, Lambis found that it ran parallel to their support lines and, at a junction in the area of the Australian attack, turned away from the front, cutting through the corner of a small wood just north of Fromelles before climbing a short rise to the town itself. This seemed to be a good place to start looking.

The next step was to obtain aerial photographs of the battlefield to try to identify any potential mass-grave sites. When the attack was being planned, the staff at Haking's headquarters had ordered reconnaissance photos to be taken by the Royal Flying Corps, and these were now held in the archives of the Imperial War Museum in London. These were the same photos that wrongly identified two lines of shallow ditches as second and third lines of German trenches. During the battle, many Australians pushed deeper into German territory with the express purpose of taking these false trenches and were doomed to die there. Ironically, the photos that led to so many casualties in 1916 ended up providing vital evidence decades later in the hunt for the mass graves.

Lambis ordered copies of these photographs and any others that might have been taken in the months either side of the battle. When the aerials arrived, he pounced on an intriguing anomaly on a post-battle image. Adjacent to the light railway and on the southern edge of the little wood it passed through, there appeared to be eight freshly dug pits in two rows of four. Eagerly, he compared it to a pre-battle aerial image, and sure enough there was no sign of excavations at the same location.

A further series of photographs obtained from the Imperial War Museum were images taken at the end of the war. They revealed that five of these pits had been backfilled soon after the battle while three remained open and apparently empty. His excitement building, Lambis wondered if they might be the mass graves mentioned by Barry, but he knew he needed more evidence before he could take his findings to the authorities.

Then came a series of breakthroughs that convinced Lambis beyond doubt that he was on the right track. Trawling through the Australian Red Cross Wounded and Missing collection at the Australian War Memorial, he found himself focusing on those files directly relating to the missing men of Fromelles. Simultaneously, he was studying the research conducted by Robin Corfield for his book. In both archives, he happened across references to Lieutenant Jack Bowden who was buried 'in one of five large British collective graves before the Fasanen Waldchen'. He looked for this location on the German trench maps produced during the war and soon found it. Triumphantly, he identified Fasanen Waldchen as the name of the very same small wood next to which he had found the eight freshly dug pits from the aerial photographs. When he translated its name into English, he learned it was known as 'Pheasants Wood'.

Now of the belief that he had enough circumstantial evidence to sustain a reasonable case, Lambis took his findings to all the relevant government departments, including the Department of Defence, Office of Australian War Graves, Army History Unit and Department of Veterans' Affairs. The response was door after door shutting firmly in his face and the strong sense that these people believed Lambis was just another crackpot with a theory. However, a man of Lambis's patience and determination was not going to be dismissed so easily, and he turned to the media with his story.

In mid-2003 articles began to appear in national newspapers about the work of Lambis and his team. Mounting pressure on the government to act led to a response from the Director of the Office of Australian War Graves, Vice Marshal Gary Beck, who requested that Lambis let the matter drop. He was firmly of the mind that no such mass graves ever existed, and, even if they had, the bodies would have been cleared after the war by the Grave Recovery Units. It must have appeared preposterous that an amateur sleuth could possibly know more than they did themselves. In his response, Beck also referred to the list of names compiled by Lambis of those he believed buried at Pheasant Wood. In doing so, the head of the Office of Australian War Graves displayed his complete misunderstanding of the nature of VC Corner Cemetery: 'Every one of those names is listed as buried at VC Corner Australian Cemetery Fromelles . . .'

While acknowledging that the 410 men buried at VC Corner had never been identified, Beck seemed to think that because all the names Lambis suggested were inscribed on the memorial wall at the cemetery, then they must be among the unnamed soldiers buried in the grounds. Without wanting to labour the point, the simplest arithmetic is enough to demonstrate that it was impossible for all of the 1299 men listed on the memorial wall to be among the 410 unknown soldiers buried there.

Lambis continued to hunt for further evidence, all the while attracting greater interest and support for his cause from both the public and media. Significantly, he also drew the attention of the federal government. In early 2005, the Opposition spokesman on veterans' affairs, Senator Mark Bishop, put pressure on the Minister for Defence, Robert Hill, to provide accurate figures on the Fromelles dead. Hill formally requested that the Office of Australian War Graves conduct an accounting of the number of Australian missing against the number of unknown graves in the surrounding cemeteries.

The results that Gary Beck returned to Minister Hill stated that of the 1299 men named on the memorial at VC Corner Cemetery, only 1136 could be accounted for, leaving 163 who appeared to have been collected and buried by the Germans. A little short of his original 'guesstimate' of 250, Lambis had since found the Australian Red Cross records and from these was able to revise his figure with greater accuracy. The number he arrived at was only two shy of Beck's, at 161.

On into 2005 Lambis and his team, the media and Senator Bishop continued to pressure the government for an examination of the Pheasant Wood site. They were buoyed to learn that Lieutenant General Peter Leahy, the chief of army, had decided to scrutinise the gathered research and would be prepared to seek permission to investigate the location should the evidence warrant it.

Ever so slowly, the tide was beginning to turn.

In June 2005 the government finally agreed to convene a Panel of Investigation. Perhaps it was hoped that granting Lambis an opportunity to be heard would stifle his increasingly vocal supporters and the whole embarrassing mess might go away.

Chaired by Roger Lee of the Army History Unit, the panel comprised a number of eminent authorities and department representatives including Professor Bill Gammage, noted author and historian at the Australian National University; Dr Bruce Scates from the University of New South Wales; Associate Professor Iain Spence from the University of New England; Professor Jeremy Grey from the Australian Defence Force Academy; Dr Peter Stanley, Craig Tibbetts and Greg Pratten of the Australian War Memorial; Air Vice-Marshal Gary Beck and Kathy Upton-Mitchell from the Office of Australian War Graves; Keith Knight from the Defence Imagery and Geospatial Organisation; Bill Houston, Brian Manns and Emma Robertson from the Army History Unit; and, last but not least, Dr John Williams, acting as an independent expert.

The intention of the panel, in short, was to assess the claims presented by Lambis and determine whether there was sufficient and compelling evidence to justify a further official investigation of the Pheasant Wood site.

In the weeks leading up to this event, Lambis and his team gathered all their evidence and fashioned it into a structured presentation of the relevant facts. They were careful not to get bogged down in details or repeat themselves unnecessarily. A PowerPoint slideshow was prepared to guide the members of the panel through the key points, and it formed a very persuasive argument. Lambis was quietly confident, but in the back of his mind he knew there were no guarantees.

The meeting opened with Roger Lee, who outlined the terms of reference and finished with a note of caution about the gravity of the potential outcome and the precedent it might set. Lambis was then invited to speak, and the room fell silent with expectation. He knew he was going to have to be good. Very good.

First, Lambis went through the numbers and emphasised that the figure of 163 that Gary Beck arrived at was very close to the 161 he himself had totalled in his search of the Red Cross records. Then, using the same Red Cross files, he referred to the important clue in the information about the burial of Lieutenant Jack Bowden and the five collective graves before 'Fasanen Waldchen'. Cross-referencing this with the German death voucher in Bowden's service file, Robin Corfield's research and the mention of the very same collective graves in the Bavarian Reserve Infantry regimental history, Lambis established a solid foundation for his case.

The oblique aerial photograph of the battlefield taken during the war was a marvellous exhibit for painting a picture of events. It clearly depicted the Australian and German trenches, and took in a view of the Sugarloaf Salient, Fromelles, the German light railway and Pheasant Wood. Moving on to the German light railway, he produced photographs and explained the regular use of this system for the removal of bodies. A compelling German caption to one of these images described the scene: 'Casualties of the battle of 19/20 July 1916. Bodies of dead English are taken from Fromelles to Fournes by field railway.'

Lambis saved his best until last. Producing German trench maps and the aerial photographs taken by the Royal Flying Corps, he was able to connect the appearance of the eight pits post-engagement and the subsequent backfilling of five of them with the wood known as Fasanen Waldchen. In this way, they were logically linked to the five collective graves mentioned in Bowden's file.

In closing, Lambis turned his attention to the efforts of the Grave Recovery Units after the war. It had long been the contention of some members of the panel that if the mass graves existed, they would have been found and exhumed soon after the armistice. Lambis was able to counter that argument with the revelation that he had personally requested that the Commonwealth War Graves Commission search the records of all the cemeteries surrounding Fromelles. The Graves Recovery Units maintained meticulous files regarding the precise location of found remains, and if any had been located at the Pheasant Wood site, the accompanying map reference would have indicated this beyond doubt.

There were none. In fact, for the entire 2 square kilometres around Pheasant Wood, the Commonwealth War Graves Commission reported that there had been 'nil returns'.

With that, the presentation was over. Lambis hoped he'd produced enough evidence to convince the panel that his claims could no longer be ignored, but he knew he was up against some heavy scepticism. Whatever the outcome, he was satisfied he'd given his all; now he could only wait. The members of the panel retired to examine the information that had been put before them. When they reached a decision, they would forward a submission to the Minister of Veterans' Affairs, De-Anne Kelly.

Just over two months later, Lambis received the panel's response. Prepared for a verdict either way, he was disappointed to learn that the recommendation was somewhat indifferent. In a distinctly negative tone, the panel had decided that the case warranted further research before any scientific examination of the site could be justified:

> *The Panel was of the view that, while not convincing, there is sufficient doubt to warrant further documentary research. It posed two questions that it considers need to be resolved before any further action should be taken. Clearer evidence is needed that the Bavarian Division did use pits or mass graves to deal with the dead from the Battle of Fromelles and that, if they did, the site you have identified is indeed the site they used. If there was a mass grave, what evidence is there that it was not found and all remains in it recovered and re-interred in the numerous war cemeteries in the area after the cessation of hostilities.*

Frustrated by the lukewarm reaction, Lambis declared that he had nevertheless made progress. Despite the doubts of some panel members, they had been forced to recognise that he had a strong circumstantial case which they couldn't readily refute. But, rather than accede to his request for an examination of the site, they wanted more proof and referred their questions to the army and Commonwealth War Graves Commission.

Not prepared to wait, and frankly incapable of sitting on his hands for that long, Lambis and his team set about finding the additional proof themselves, scouring through the material yet again. It was while re-examining the war-graves records that they stumbled upon the names of soldiers killed at Fromelles who, by a quirk of fate, had been omitted from the VC Corner Memorial and instead named on the Villers-Bretonneux Memorial.

Among them was Lieutenant Robert Burns, who had already been determined by Major Allen of the Australian Graves Service to be buried at Fournes. Fortuitously, the account of Allen's search around Fromelles had been documented in the Court of Enquiry transcript and in his own words provided solid proof that, although Pheasant Wood had been searched after the war, no mass graves had been located as late as 1920.

The importance of this discovery was immediately recognised by Lambis. If the graves had not been found prior to 1920, then it was almost certain that they had never been detected at all and that the bodies would still be there undisturbed.

Enter Chris Bryett.

A Sydney lawyer and avid amateur Australian military historian, Chris would have a crucial influence on the outcome of the Pheasant Wood enquiry. Labelled a 'cowboy' by some, the approach he eventually took to resolving the issue was very different from the well-worn path trodden by Lambis. Rather than following a long-drawn-out bureaucratic procedure, Chris decided that the government needed to be shaken up. In the end, the combination of Lambis politely knocking on the front door with irrefutable evidence and Chris pounding holes through the back wall with a sledgehammer was ultimately to prove most effective.

Chris first saw Pheasant Wood mentioned on an internet forum. His curiosity aroused, he continued to follow the case as it developed in the media. It was only after touring the Western Front in early 2006 and visiting Pheasant Wood that he felt stirred into action, and upon his return he personally contacted Lambis. To begin with, Chris joined the core group of amateur historians and worked in tandem with Lambis, but it wasn't long before the lawyer lost patience with a government that was dragging its heels on the issue. He was convinced there had to be a quicker way of getting things done.

When the Williams Report was tabled to the Panel of Investigation in 2006, Chris's frustration turned to downright disillusionment. He decided enough was enough. Panel member Dr John Williams was the independent expert assessing the evidence put forward by Lambis. A published author with several degrees under his belt, including a PhD in Modern History from Macquarie University, Williams had travelled to Fromelles to conduct enquiries as a consequence of the panel's findings.

For some unfathomable reason, Williams decided that the eight pits dug on the outskirts of Pheasant Wood had been prepared 'before' the battle. He then argued it was unlikely that German troops would have been spared to dig burial pits in the lead-up to a battle, so they were more likely to be defensive positions for German trench mortars. His only concession to the Pheasant Wood graves' existence was that they might contain the bodies of a few Portuguese soldiers killed in 1918 and buried in the mortar pits after the weapons had been moved elsewhere.

It seems Williams based his theory on an old German map shown to him by a French historian he had visited during his investigations. This map purportedly depicted war graves dug by the Germans in the Fromelles area but there was nothing on it to indicate the existence of mass graves in the vicinity of Pheasant Wood. He had absolutely no evidence to suggest that the pits were dug prior to the battle, and what he had failed to ascertain was whether the map showed the locations of all graves dug by the Germans throughout the period of the war, or only those they had prepared for their own dead. Indeed, it has never been established what the original purpose of the map was, so it should not have been used for anything other than idle speculation.

Strewn with largely baseless assumptions, Williams' report was submitted to the panel. When Chris Bryett obtained a copy, he could barely contain his fury. He was convinced that, left to the bureaucrats, the matter would no doubt grind on interminably, so he decided to take things into his own hands. If the government refused to act, then he would.

Over the coming months, he began building his own team of experts. His plan was to engage the services of the most eminent professionals in their respective fields, take them to Pheasant Wood and find the missing soldiers by themselves. Naming the venture 'Recovering Overseas Australia's Missing', or ROAM for short, Chris obtained the assistance of a number of well-respected experts. The team was made up of Richard

Wright, emeritus professor of Anthropology at the University of Sydney, who had recently investigated the mass graves in Bosnia and Croatia and was considered a world leader in the field; Jon Stereneberg, the director of excavations and examinations for the International Commission on Missing Persons in Bosnia, who arranged for a sample series of tests should DNA be acquired; Alan Cooper from the Centre for Ancient DNA in Adelaide; British archaeologist Martin Brown, who was known for his appearances in several Great War archaeological television programs and was also an adviser to the British All Party Parliamentary War Graves and Battlefield Heritage Group; Warrant Officer Rod Scott, whose knowledge of Great War ordnance was virtually second to none; and, finally, Mike Kelly, tour guide and historian with years of practical experience in France.

With financial backing from a former soldier turned mining businessman, George Jones, ROAM was finally ready to go public. Catching everyone by surprise, Chris announced ROAM's intentions. The audacious proposal was initially met with derision from government representatives, but it soon became evident that Chris had done his homework and could counter their disapproval with evidence of the enormous amount of preparation he had already put in. Despite their best efforts, clearly no one from the panel was going to be able to divert Chris's ambitions. What's more, they began to realise that he had put together a seriously professional group with a well-structured plan, and, given Chris had tentatively obtained necessary permission from French officials and the landowner, there was little they could do to stop him acting independently.

And then came news of an extraordinary discovery of long-neglected documents in the Munich War Archive, which presented two more vital pieces of the puzzle. The first document was a copy of the order by Major General Julius Ritter von Braun that mentioned, 'The bodies of English soldiers are being interred in mass graves directly south of Pheasants Wood.' The second was an entry in the 21st Bavarian Reserve Infantry Regiment War Diary: 'For the enemy dead, mass graves are being constructed behind Fasanen Waldchen.'

These records, providing clear evidence that the graves at Pheasant Wood had existed, gave the Panel of Investigation acceptable reason to re-evaluate their original findings and save the situation from descending into a very public farce. They were well aware that private individuals excavating possible grave sites could seriously undermine their authority and knew they must avoid any potential damage and embarrassment in allowing such a precedent to be set. In a sudden but not unexpected turnaround, they recommended that the minister authorise an evaluation of the Pheasant Wood site.

Although the panel ostensibly based their decision on the new evidence before them, there can be no doubt that without the dogged persistence of Lambis Englezos and the sheer brazen front of Chris Bryett, they might not have reacted quite so quickly. Indeed, the recommendations to the minister had a decidedly negative tone, as we can see from the three findings:

- Although not agreed by all panel members, the majority accepted that the evidence suggested Australian soldiers had been buried in mass graves behind Pheasant Wood.
- Evidence to suggest the soldiers had not later been exhumed and reburied elsewhere was circumstantial and insufficient to justify an excavation of the site.
- Because the evidence proving the soldiers still remained in the mass graves was inadequate, only a non-invasive survey of the site would be conducted to establish whether a further physical examination was warranted.

It was a (cautious) step in the right direction, and Team Lambis could be satisfied that their persistence had achieved a measure of success. Everything now depended on the results of the non-invasive survey.

Chapter 7

DUST AND METAL

The non-invasive survey of the site established beyond doubt that Australian troops at least had been buried on the site and also provided quite compelling evidence that the graves had not been discovered after the war and were therefore intact and undisturbed.

GUARD Pheasant Wood Fromelles Data Structure Report, 2008

Chris Bryett had every reason to believe that ROAM, with its wealth of expertise and a track record of experience on the matter, would offer the best geophysical survey of the Pheasant Wood site. He was therefore surprised and disappointed to learn that Dr Tony Pollard and the Glasgow University Archaeological Research Division (GUARD) had been engaged for the task. On the one hand, he had helped the process by bullying the authorities into action, but on the other he had inevitably hampered ROAM's chances of playing an official role.

There were also rumours circulating that he had made misrepresentations to the French authorities in order to gain permission for an archaeological dig by claiming he had

Australian Government support, so that didn't help his case. Flatly denied by Chris and in truth probably more of a misunderstanding than a deliberate attempt at deception, it still made ROAM's participation too much of a political liability.

Under the watchful eye of Lambis Englezos (who arrived in Fromelles a few days earlier) for two weeks in May 2007, Pollard and his GUARD team meticulously combed the Pheasant Wood site using non-invasive survey techniques. These included topographical testing to reveal any changes related to the pits, resistivity to recognise archaeological features beneath the soil, ground-penetrating radar to provide depth analysis, and metal-detecting to locate surface artefacts and determine their spread pattern.

Dr Tony Pollard is an internationally renowned archaeologist specialising in the archaeology of conflict and the director of the Centre for Battlefield Archaeology at Glasgow University, but he is probably best known to the masses as co-presenter of the BBC series *Two Men in a Trench*, a popular history program exploring famous battle-scenes. Pollard's brief from the Australian authorities was, in short, to confirm the existence of the pits, estimate their size and condition, and establish the likelihood of them still containing the buried remains of soldiers.

Using Lambis's evidence and corroborating it with their own archival research, GUARD initially established that the wood and surrounding features were virtually unchanged since the Great War. Then, methodically criss-crossing the area with their equipment, they gradually gathered the data that would enable them to accurately chronicle the site's existence over the intervening years. When the work was complete, the GUARD team retired to analyse the results.

Back in Australia, all those involved in the campaign and the relatives of those still missing waited anxiously. The final resolution of ancient family tragedies depended on the outcome, not to mention the tangible desire to validate years of voluntary labour carried out by Lambis and his team. When the report was finally delivered by Tony Pollard in mid-July 2008, you could almost hear a collective sigh of relief as the last vestiges of doubt dissolved. GUARD's findings revealed not only that the graves had existed but also that the evidence strongly suggested that the ground had not been disturbed since 1916, with the bodies probably fully *in situ*.

The topographical survey revealed a series of slight depressions and ridges in the ground surface corresponding to the eight backfilled pits, as well as the former German light-railway line running adjacent to the site. This was reinforced by the geophysical survey, which identified only weak irregularities corresponding to the pit arrangement. Had the pits been excavated post-war and then refilled, this survey would have resulted in much stronger readings. The radar survey heightened the detail of each individual pit and provided an estimate of between 2- to 2.5-metre depths.

It was the metal detector, however, that was the star of the show. Because of the enormity of the Great War and the industrial scale on which it was waged, this simple device usually provides only limited scope for use in Great War archaeology, and is more of a relic-hunter's tool, but because of the defined nature of the area in this case, it was thought worthwhile. Results indicated British shrapnel evenly spread around the site as well as in the upper layer of fill in the pits. Most likely a result of the final British assault, the presence of shrapnel just under the surface of the graves strongly indicated that they had not been excavated after the war, because the shrapnel would have been disturbed.

However, the two most valuable finds by the metal detectors proved beyond doubt the presence of Australians at Pheasant Wood. During the sweep of the site, the soil yielded two small metal medallions right next to the pits. The first of these medallions was embossed with the word 'ANZAC' (Australian and New Zealand Army Corps), and, although there was no way to identify the owner, it had clearly belonged to an Australian soldier. The second medallion was even more promising. Made from a copper alloy, it was slightly concave and had remnants of red, white and blue enamel still adhering to its face. Imprinted in large lettering at the centre was 'AIF', and the lucky-horse-shoe surround carried the words 'SHIRE OF ALBERTON'. At the tips of the horseshoe were the dates '1914' and '1915' respectively, and across the base was a scroll containing a par-tially illegible motto: 'FOR . . .' Evidently a good-luck charm from a local shire somewhere in Australia, it caught the eye of one of Lambis's closest supporters, Tim Whitford, who had come on board in 2006.

When Tim read about the discovery of the medallion, he was immediately struck by the fact that it was from Alberton, and from then on it became his personal project to research its origins in the hope of identifying the original owner.

Tim's great-uncle, 983 Private Henry Willis (his family called him Harry) of the 31st Battalion, was among the missing men believed buried at Pheasant Wood, and he had been born in the rural Victorian town of Alberton. Tim immediately entertained the slim possibility that it might have belonged to Harry, but, tempting as the coincidence might be, a search of more than just a cursory nature was needed to verify it.

To begin with, there was a suggestion that Vic Momplhait could also have been a contender, as he originally hailed from Alberton in South Australia. But he was soon ruled out when it was discovered that Alberton, South Australia, was a suburb of Port Adelaide and had never been part of an administrative shire by that name. Tim was able to confirm that there had only ever been one area of Australia known by that particular shire name, and that the owner of the medallion must somehow be linked to it.

Located in South Gippsland, Alberton lent its name to the local administrative council the Shire of Alberton, an area nestled between the Strzelecki Ranges and Victoria's coastline. Now amalgamated into the larger Wellington Shire, the seat of the former Shire of Alberton was the town of Yarram, but within its boundaries was also to be found a number of other communities, including Port Albert, Alberton, Tarraville, Macks Creek and Binginwarri among others. According to author John Adams in his book *From These Beginnings: History of the Shire of Alberton*, over 800 men from the district enlisted for service during the Great War. Of this number, seventy-four are listed on the Yarram war memorial as killed in service.

First, Tim had to prove the existence of such a medallion. Turning to the archives of the *Gippsland Standard* newspaper, he located a wealth of primary-source information printed during the war, including many articles farewelling soldiers and mentioning the presentation of shire medallions:

2 November 1915

Private H.S. Davis was met at the shire hall on Friday morning by a few townsmen and presented with the usual card and medallion by Mr V.S. Lalor.

19 November 1915

He presented the soldiers with a card and medallion and expressed a wish that their friends would see them again wearing the medals.

5 April 1916

On behalf of the people of the Shire of Alberton, he had the pleasure of presenting to each a medallion and card, with all good wishes . . . Mr T.G. McKenzie responded on behalf of the soldiers and expressed their appreciation of the sentiments uttered in the medallion and cards.

5 May 1916

Cr. Barlow then presented the Alberton Shire Medals.

These medallions appeared to be a way of recognising every man who enlisted in the district, and they were presented to soldiers in a ceremony just prior to their departure for war service. According to newspaper reports, these ceremonies were normally well attended and consisted of speeches made by local dignitaries before the medallions were issued with the accompanying card.

After the war, local memorials began to spring up in almost every town around the country, and the Shire of Alberton was no different. In February 1920 the shire secretary, Mr G. W. Black, placed a notice in the *Gippsland Standard* asking for names to be submitted for a roll of honour:

> *The undersigned would be pleased to receive the names of men who enlisted from the Shire and went overseas on active service, or who were in camp on the signing of the Armistice preparing for active service . . . The names of those who received the Shire Medallion are not required as a list of them has been compiled.*

It was interesting that this notice pointed out that not all soldiers of the district received a medallion, so Tim's next task was to find out the context in which it was issued. With the assistance of the Wellington Shire archivist, Kay Paterson, Tim began scouring the Shire of Alberton archives. Although no wartime references to the medallion could be found in shire documentation, a considerable quantity of correspondence was located in reply to the 1920 newspaper announcement calling for the submission of names for the roll of honour. These letters coincidentally told much about the circumstances in which the medallions were issued.

In his letter of response to the shire secretary, 1566 Lance Corporal James Lindsay suggested that soldiers who enlisted early in the war did not appear to have received medallions: 'I have not yet received my Shire Medallion; so thought perhaps you have not got my name for the Roll of Honour. I went into camp in 1914 before you were giving these medallions to the soldiers.' This is backed up by the fact that the earliest mention of the medallion appeared in the local paper in 1915, so it seems that the men who enlisted the year before missed out. In all likelihood, the medallion was probably still in the concept phase.

Other letters implied that medallions were only issued to soldiers who enlisted within the shire itself. Written in March 1920, one of these letters was a goldmine of information for Tim. Written by Janet Willis, Harry's mother, not only did it verify that if a local man enlisted elsewhere he did not receive the medallion, it also confirmed that Harry Willis had indeed been issued with one: 'Four of my sons received the Shire Medallion but my son Charles Robert Willis enlisted in Swan Hill and did not receive one here. As he is a native of Alberton, I thought I would send his name in also.'

After the appearance of an article in a local newspaper about the Fromelles investigation and Tim's ongoing research into the medallion, the daughter of a soldier who had received one contacted him. She still had her father's medallion in her possession, and she invited Tim to come and inspect it. To his delight, it was virtually identical to the one recovered at Pheasant Wood, except that it was understandably in far better condition.

The woman explained that her father had received his medallion upon enlistment, and she then produced the small prayer card that had accompanied it. Tim was now able to complete the motto that was almost completely illegible on the recovered medallion: 'FOR DUTY DONE'. The provenance couldn't be any better and proved that the recovered medallion irrefutably belonged to a soldier from the Alberton Shire district of Victoria.

Turning now to the military archives, Tim examined personnel files, embarkation lists and Red Cross Enquiry Files to identify soldiers from the Shire of Alberton who were killed at Fromelles and therefore potentially buried at Pheasant Wood. He located only four possible men with links to the shire.

1168 Corporal David Livingston of the 29th Battalion was born at Tarraville in the Shire of Alberton. His service file revealed that he was killed at Fromelles and that his remains likely fell into German hands. Based on his Red Cross Enquiry File and the corresponding German death list documentation, it appeared he was quite possibly one of those buried at the Pheasant Wood site. However, his records also showed that he enlisted in the northern Victorian border town of Kerang, over 500 kilometres from the shire boundary. He later took his medical examination at Barham in New South Wales, so he clearly fell into the category of not qualifying for a medallion due to his distance from the shire upon enlistment. In addition, Corporal Livingston's enlistment occurred in early November 1914 and therefore pre-dated the creation and presentation of the first recorded medallions. Although there is an exceptionally slim chance that Corporal Livingston possessed a medallion, it remains extremely unlikely that the one recovered at Pheasant Wood was his.

A member of the 59th Battalion, 4130 Private Isaac Lear was positioned at the opposite end of the advancing Australian line to David Livingston. Born at Tarraville, Lear was a local bootmaker living with his mother in Yarram at the time of his enlistment. In his service file was a letter dated 1921 from his mother to the Army Base Records Office regarding the hopeful recovery of his remains. It confirms that Lear had been one of the district's soldiers to be issued with a Shire of Alberton medallion: 'This is all the information I can give with the exception of a few articles that I am sure would be on his person should he be recovered without an identification disc. 1 shire medallion medal blue enamel, presented by Alberton Shire (Gippsland), for duty done.'

However, Lear was involved in the attack on the Sugarloaf Salient, and the vast majority of those men never made it to the German lines. In the same letter, she describes his death as it was explained to her by one of his mates who witnessed it: 'He [Long] was with my son, advancing with fixed bayonets. After abandoning the lewis gun they were carrying and were tired of, they crossed a gully only to get on level ground and my son was shot in the throat.' Most importantly, she makes a further reference to the Alberton medallion and a unique feature that distinguishes her son's from any other: 'The medal was initialed I.J.L. on the rear.' The medallion recovered at Pheasant Wood had no inscription of any kind on its rear face and is therefore almost certainly not the one belonging to Isaac Lear.

2641 Private Herbert Gilfoy was born in Lincolnshire, England, but he migrated to Australia and was working as a farm labourer in the Shire of Alberton when he enlisted at Yarram in 1915. There is every reason to believe he would have been presented with a medallion prior to his departure. He was assigned to the 59th Battalion alongside Isaac Lear and, during the battle, also took part in the assault against the Sugarloaf Salient. Receiving a gunshot wound to the head during the battle, he was rescued from no-man's-land but succumbed to his injuries a few days later at the 30th General Hospital in Calais. An inventory of the personal effects returned to his father in Lincolnshire, England, and recorded in his service file revealed the following items: disc, letters, wallet, note case, belt, pipe, wooden cross, cufflinks, photos and pencil case. No shire medallion appears to have been in his possession at the time nor returned with his other belongings. If we were to go so far as to make the assumption that Herbert Gilfoy was actually carrying his medallion at the time of his wounding, the fact that he died in an Allied hospital a long way from the battlefield and far from the hands of the enemy would make the finding of his medallion at Pheasant Wood implausible if not totally impossible.

The last soldier identified by Tim as likely to have been in possession of an Alberton medallion at the time of death was his great-uncle, Harry Willis. He had already established that Harry had been issued with a medallion and, like Livingston, both his Red Cross Enquiry File and personnel records contained the German documentation that strongly indicated he had been buried at Pheasant Wood. But, unlike the other three, there was not a single inconsistency in his file to suggest that the medallion unearthed at Pheasant Wood might not be his. Indeed, when comparing the likely chances of these four men being the owner of the recovered medallion, Harry Willis was the front-runner by a country mile.

Finally, it dawned on Tim that the scrap of metal he held in his hand was almost certainly the last-known physical link to his lost ancestor. His goal was tantalisingly close, but he knew there was still no assurance of success. The difference was that, now more than ever, Tim Whitford was committed to fulfilling the promise he had made to his family: he was going to find their uncle Harry.

Chapter 8
SHERLOCK AND MARPLE

We all grow up with the weight of history on us. Our ancestors dwell in our minds as they do in the spiralling chains of knowledge hidden in every cell of our bodies.

From *Womenfolks: Growing Up Down South* by Shirley Abbott

My own serious involvement in the Fromelles project began in November 2007.

Over the years, I had made many contacts in both the genealogical and the Great War research communities, and it was through these connections that I first learned about Lambis Englezos and his quest. In around 2004, I emailed him a letter of support as an interested onlooker, and Lambis responded with a compelling account of what he was doing. I was hooked. I keenly followed his efforts for several years and received periodic updates from him as events unfolded.

However, it wasn't until I attended a book launch at the Hellenic RSL in South Melbourne for Patrick Lindsay's work on Fromelles that we actually met for the first time. As Lambis described the battle and the subsequent trail of his research to the assembled gathering, I found myself captivated by the narrative and increasingly frustrated at the indifference shown by the authorities.

The key moment for me was when a member of the audience gave an impromptu address. Sitting quietly and attentively throughout the evening's formal presentations, Major General Mike O'Brien was recognised by Lambis, whereupon he was introduced to the meeting and invited to say a few words. A career soldier in the Australian Army, Mike O'Brien graduated from Duntroon in 1968 and was allocated to the Royal Australian Infantry Corps. He served as a platoon commander and intelligence officer of 7th Battalion, Royal Australian Regiment, in Vietnam from 1970 to 1971, after which he held a variety of instructional and project-management positions. A recipient of the Conspicuous Service Cross, he is also a graduate of the Australian Staff College, the Australian College of Defence and Strategic Studies, the Royal Military College of Science (UK), the University of New South Wales and Cranfield University (UK).

Mike retired from the army in 2002 but was re-engaged in 2007 to play a significant role in the recovery, identification and reburial of five Australian soldiers killed during the Third Battle of Ypres. The remains of these men, commonly known as the 'Zonnebeke Five', had been discovered in the course of earthworks near Polygon Wood, close to the Belgian village of Westhoek, in September 2006. In an investigation not unlike Fromelles, except on a much smaller scale, four of the five Australians were successfully identified by a combination of historical research and modern scientific analysis. Crucially, this included a precedent for the use of DNA technology in Great War battlefield recoveries. During an interview about his involvement in the efforts to identify these five men, Mike O'Brien commented:

> We don't always have the capacity to recover DNA from the remains, or the capacity to match it with relatives, but we make every effort to do so and I think that's very important. It's carrying on a job that really started during the First World War and particularly after it when the Graves Recoveries Unit got these soldiers and made their best efforts to identify them. We feel it's our job still, and I think it's very important for the relatives particularly.

Fresh from representing the chief of army at the burial service in Belgium for the Zonnebeke Five two months earlier, Mike O'Brien now stood before the audience in South Melbourne and told us about his experiences.

He was careful to remind everyone about the moral, ethical and scientific considerations, and went on to suggest how the technology might be applied to the Fromelles case. Then came the surprise announcement that he had just been engaged to head the Department of Defence's 'Australian Fromelles Project Group' (AFPG). This organisation, he told us, had recently been assembled to investigate the mass graves suspected to exist at Pheasant Wood and to determine what action should be taken if they were found to contain the remains of Australian soldiers. For Lambis, this was a light at the end of a very long tunnel. For me, the seed of an idea was planted.

I realised they would need an enormous amount of input from descendants to help identify any Australians recovered, and a genealogy project would fit the bill. The first requirement would be putting names to those men potentially buried at the Pheasant Wood site. Follow-up research would then have to be carried out on each soldier's family tree with a view to procuring DNA matches.

My mind whirring with possibilities, I mentioned my initiative briefly to Lambis that night and later approached Mike O'Brien on the front steps of the RSL as we were leaving. He cautioned me that there was still much to be done and many considerations to be taken into account, but he agreed that there would certainly be a need for the work I proposed, should subsequent investigations take us along that route.

In the following years, I had a good deal of contact with Mike O'Brien and the AFPG. Although we occasionally crossed swords over the fine line between contracted professionals and gifted amateurs, there can be no question of his absolute commitment to the men who had been buried at Pheasant Wood, nor his unwavering determination to ensure they were treated with the utmost respect and honour. He was most certainly the right man for the job.

The next day, I contacted my research partner, Sandra Playle, in Western Australia and told her to put all our other research on hold. Puzzled at first, she soon became very interested when I explained that we were about to embark on a volunteer project that would involve examining the files of more than 2000 Australian soldiers killed at Fromelles. Our aim would be to single out those men who might potentially be buried in the mass graves at Pheasant Wood. We would compile family trees for each of those identified, and then work forward in time to locate living descendants. It was a tall order, but, unable to resist a challenge of this magnitude, Sandra committed to the proposal without hesitation, and the 'Fromelles Descendant Database' project was born.

Like me, Sandra had felt drawn towards studying history and from a young age was particularly interested in her family's origins. Born in Geraldton, she grew up in the remote town of Yalgoo in Western Australia. Sandra did well at school, but her fierce streak of independence showed through when, at the age of fifteen, she took herself out of the system and continued her studies by correspondence. An avid non-fiction reader, she was drawn to books about history, true crime and espionage, and loved the crime-solving aspect of mystery novels. As a young adult, the demands of a growing family and her job in administration took her away from study, but she returned to TAFE and then university, where she focused on Policy Studies, particularly excelling in the subjects of demography and qualitative research.

In 1980 her cousin published a version of their family tree, but only from the time their ancestors arrived in Australia. This was not enough to satisfy Sandra's curiosity and she began researching beyond Australia's shores to locate the Playles' ancestral home. As she painstakingly traced the line of her fore-bears, Sandra discovered an instinctual aptitude for genealogy and before long had established herself within the international genealogical-research community. She even started her own pri-vate service offering assistance to others.

During her personal research, Sandra learned that her grand-father had served during the Great War, along with several great-uncles and cousins on either side of her family. She was quite affected to learn that two of them never returned from the battlefields. The stories of her ancestors' service introduced her to Australia's military heritage, and her ongoing campaign to protect the memory of this country's servicemen can be directly attrib-uted to the influence of her own family's sacrifice so long ago.

Sandra is particularly interested in cemeteries and, over the years, has photographed and documented a large num-ber of them in her home state. On a trip to visit relatives in Albany one year, she decided to photograph the heritage-listed Memorial Park Cemetery, which happened to be the very first consecrated cemetery in Western Australia. Reading the many memorials to young soldiers struck a chord with Sandra, and later she returned on another trip to photograph the memorial plaques in Albany's Avenue of Honour, which leads up to the Desert Mounted Corps memorial atop Mount Clarence.

Overlooking King George Sound, where all the troopships had lain at anchor before heading off to war, Mount Clarence was the last glimpse of home for many young Australians. As Sandra stood gazing across the waters of the sound, the names and ages of those men who were destined never to see Australian shores again reeled off in her mind. Unable to shake off a profound feeling of loss, and embracing the ethos that 'every soldier earns the right to live forever', Sandra made a silent pact to recover their identities. So began her research to reveal the lives and deaths of some 1300 soldiers associated with the Albany area. The study took several years to complete and forms the most comprehensive source of personal information about the young men from Albany who volunteered to serve during the Great War. Upon its completion, Sandra donated the publication to the City of Albany Local Studies Library.

In 2000 Sandra embarked upon a Bachelor of Arts with a postgraduate degree in Social Research and Evaluation. She also found time to campaign against the removal and destruction of the Commonwealth War Graves headstones during site renewal at the Karrakatta Cemetery in Perth. It was while she was fighting to protect these precious monuments that Sandra first came into contact with Lambis and his crusade to find the missing men at Fromelles.

Sandra and I first became acquainted in 2005 through a number of online Great War and genealogical forums. With very similar interests, we often found ourselves engaging in the same discussions and adding our respective knowledge to identical research topics. Acknowledging our common preoccupations, we began regularly assisting with each other's work. Where Sandra had her grounding in genealogical studies, coming later to focus her skills on military research, my foundation was precisely the opposite, and consequently we formed a strong working partnership, each complementing and supporting the other. Before long, we formalised our association, combining our abilities to investigate our first case.

It began as an online thread on the Great War Forum, of which Sandra and I are members. The initiator was discussing a recent book he had read by the British journalist and author Robert Fisk, who recounted a disturbing event in his father's life. Bill Fisk was a British officer during the First World War who commanded a firing squad that was given the task of executing a British soldier for murder. The soldier was claiming that he was, in fact, an Australian deserter.

Fisk was aware that the British military authorities did not have permission to execute Australian soldiers after the disastrous Breaker Morant episode in the Boer War. The young soldier must have been suitably convincing because Bill risked destroying his future military career by refusing to carry out the execution. This odd story piqued our interest and we decided to do some background checking, blissfully unaware of the complex tragedy that would unfold.

Enlisting in Sydney as a sixteen-year-old, 1709 Private Richard Mellor (his real name was Samuel, but he used his older brother's name to pass the age limit) saw action in Egypt and at Gallipoli. His youthful adventure must have soured quickly, and he was hospitalised on numerous occasions with various ailments and finally declared permanently disabled, but for some reason he was not sent home. Instead, he ended up in a training camp in Wiltshire, England, from where he deserted three times before he disappeared altogether in May 1918 and was never heard of again.

Around the same time, a British recruitment drive scooped up a young man who gave his name as Frank Oswald Wills. The soldier was sent to France, where he deserted two weeks after the armistice, but he was located the following March. During his arrest in a Paris bar, the inebriated Wills shot two MPs, one of whom later died of his wounds. In his court martial, Wills made the startling admission that he was in fact an Australian national. He said that when he deserted the Australian Army, he was too afraid to reveal his identity to the British recruitment officers and so gave a false name.

Wills was sentenced to death, but he was granted his final wish to speak with an Australian officer before he was executed. During his meeting with the officer in charge of Australian troops in Paris, Major Burford Samson, the condemned man recounted with great accuracy the details of Private Richard Mellor's service and private life. He claimed he had joined the army at sixteen, fought in a number of campaigns and then suffered a terrible fever that led to permanent mental problems and memory lapses. When he joined the British troops, he fell in with the wrong crowd, drinking and gambling until his final fateful arrest. Condemned to die and knowing that nothing could save him, he requested that his mother, Elizabeth Mellor, be informed what became of him.

In the following days, a report was sent to the London headquarters of the AIF recounting the interview. Poor communication meant that Mellor/Wills had already been executed by firing squad (not commanded by Bill Fisk) by the time there was any response, but the authorities had decided not to investigate the matter anyway. Even so, a file was created for 253617 F. O. Wills. It contained only some memos requesting that 'Mrs Wills' be located and informed of her son's death. The address that was listed was the same Sydney address where Elizabeth Mellor lived. The memos were never complied with.

For years, Elizabeth Mellor wrote letters pleading for news of what had happened to her son. The last one, sent in 1939, confirmed that Elizabeth Mellor's desperation and sorrow had scarcely diminished in twenty years:

> *I had a son named Samuel Rowley Mellor . . . His number was 1709 or 709, I forget now it was so long ago, though my tears don't dry when I think of him. He joined up under the name Richard Rowley Mellor, that was his elder brother's name. He gave his age as 22 but my darling was only 17 years . . . I am now nearing the closing of life, I am 80. I would be very grateful to you for a reply.*

For Sandra and me, it was frustrating to read of her torment, knowing that the combination of a sluggish bureaucracy, embarrassed officials, the stigma of desertion and a young man's fear, shame and probable mental incapacity had robbed her of the knowledge of her son's demise. However, there is a postscript to this sad tale. The letter Elizabeth wrote in 1939 is the last one that she sent to the authorities, and yet it was another twelve years before she herself passed on. Another one of her sons (Richard) provided the details for her death certificate, naming three sons still living and two who predeceased her. The fact that it did not acknowledge the existence of a sixth son, Samuel, is a compelling indicator that somehow she finally found out that he had in fact been a deserter and, worse, had killed a man sent to arrest him and was executed for the crime. Rather than endure the public disgrace, she may well have erased him from the family history. Certainly, subsequent generations of the Mellors had no knowledge of his existence.

It gave us mixed feelings to contemplate that although Elizabeth Mellor may well have received closure in her last years, it was not the kind of closure that would bring a mother comfort.

The case is a fine example of the level of difficulty we regularly encounter in our work when gaping holes in primary evidence and the eroding passage of time pose seemingly insurmountable challenges. Revealing the tragic circumstances of this young soldier was our first official collaboration, and his story is one that neither of us will ever forget.

Sandra and I live on opposite sides of the country, so we have relied heavily on technology to keep in touch. At first, we did so primarily by email and phone, but Skype has far and away become our most valuable communication tool. Being able to analyse results and discuss plans and options at length (and I mean for several hours at a time!) with both verbal and visual capabilities and with all our notes close to hand has enabled our research to progress in leaps and bounds.

Generally, Sandra will prepare all the preliminary research on the family trees and any other relevant information she can glean from family-history records, websites, newspapers, military records and military websites. Time and again, it has been the military records that have provided the scrap of information that solved a mystery, so it has been a tremendous advantage that Sandra's area of expertise is military research. In the case of Leslie Leister (detailed more thoroughly in Chapter 11), it was a seemingly innocuous letter from the insurance company, kept in his service records, that gave us the vital clue to his identity. Sandra has a vast resource library, including indices of birth, baptism, marriage, death and burial certificates for both Australia and the United Kingdom. Her lounge room has been taken over by books, IT equipment, microfiche (with her own reader), piles of CDs and DVDs, files, bookcases and a mountain of paperwork. This complements our joint collection of church records, military references and a wealth of other historical data. The material that Sandra doesn't actually physically possess is usually available either online or via her vast network of genealogy research colleagues.

The internet has revolutionised the study of genealogy. Masses of information is now available on CD, DVD or online, including a surprising number of newspaper archives. Gone are the days when researchers would pick their way through dusty bookshelves and spend hours hunched over cumbersome microfiche machines in chilly library research rooms. Now, many public archives are well maintained and indexed, so if we are required to research on site, the information is relatively easy to access. (Having said that, there were instances during the Fromelles research when we had to travel interstate to get what we needed, which was a costly and time-consuming enterprise.)

There was one important resource, however, that had sadly been lost in time. The Commonwealth War Graves Commission in Berkshire, England, keep an archive of burial returns for many of their cemeteries scattered across the world. The returns tell us where a body was first recovered after the war and then reburied in an officially recognised cemetery. In certain cases, we could combine this information with other evidence to confirm identification of a set of remains. It was frustrating to learn that during a well-meant 'recycling' drive in the Second World War, some of these vital records were destroyed and the information gone forever. This proved to be a significant stumbling block in several of our cases.

Sandra's findings are then passed on to me and I apply them to more contemporary records, such as electoral lists, newspapers, telephone directories and internet data. This way, I will follow the family trail until, hopefully, it leads to a descendant.

Through it all, there is regular communication between us as we tease out problems and review different options. 'A fresh set of eyes' is a term we often use as, time and again, one of us will be thrashing about trying to solve a particular issue and the other will instantly identify what needs to be done. Objectivity is a wonderful thing.

People often ask us how we juggle the workload without stepping on each other's toes. It's a simple set-up founded on mutual respect and common goals, with very little ego coming into it. Our roles are not defined, but there is an unspoken understanding about how the tasks are divided up, based on our individual strengths and weaknesses. I have had lots of experience as a writer, speaker and negotiator, so naturally much of the direct communication with families has fallen to me, although Sandra will take over when the subjects are closer to her home state.

It helps that we've both got a dry sense of humour, and there's an easy camaraderie there too. Besides the obvious fact that I was a police officer, my ability to think laterally when solving a tricky research problem led to Sandra giving me the moniker of 'Sherlock'. In return, Sandra's extraordinary organisational skills and her almost supernatural talent for bringing obscure recorded facts to light led me to start referring to her as 'Marple'. It's now years later and the nicknames have well and truly stuck.

Once we had committed ourselves to creating the database, we had to formulate a plan to tackle the monumental task that lay ahead. Before even beginning to sift through archives and records, we needed to identify our goals and determine our terms of reference.

At this point, there was still no certainty that the remains were even going to be exhumed from the mass graves, so our first priority was to determine the names of all the Australians potentially buried at Pheasant Wood for any future recognition. Once this list had been established, our next goal was to identify living descendants of all who appeared on it. Based on the hopeful presumption that exhumation and DNA testing might indeed take place, we decided to focus this second phase of our research according to suitable DNA family lines, although both Sandra and I agreed not to limit the scope of the search to these

Oblique aerial photograph of the Fromelles battlefield *(Courtesy of AWM, item E05990)*

Australian dead in a German line at Fromelles.

The Glasgow University Archaeological Research Division compound
at Pheasant Wood. *(Courtesy of the FFFAIF)*

The Oxford Archaeology team at work on the Pheasant Wood site.
*(Courtesy of Oxford Archaeology on behalf of the Australian Army and
the UK Ministry of Defence)*

1634 Private Jack Joyce, 32nd Battalion. He is believed to have been buried at Pheasant Wood but has not yet been identified. *(Photograph courtesy of Yvonne Nye)*

Land England TotenListen Nr.		10536	/36
Name Abschrift	Joyce, J.		
Dienstgrad	Sold.	Nr. der Erk.-Marke	1624
Truppenteil	32.A.J., C.E.		
Zeit u. Ort der Gefangennahme	Erk.Marke überwesen v.N.O.A.O.K.6		
Aufenthaltsort	durch M.A.(Zentralstelle für		
Bemerkungen Verwundung Heimatsort	Nachlasssachen) 12.10.16.		

Jack Joyce's German death voucher.

The well-travelled binoculars of Major Victor Sampson, 53rd Battalion, were returned to his family in 2010. They had been salvaged by soldiers, and then used to watch horse races back in Sydney. *(Courtesy of Paul Arthur)*

Left: Bob Green died on the battlefield; his bloodstained identification disc was returned to his family in 1917. *(Courtesy of Teresa and Graham Westerling)*

Right: A surviving Shire of Alberton medallion alongside one unearthed at Pheasant Wood. *(Courtesy of Tim Whitford)*

Return train ticket from Fremantle to Perth recovered from the mass graves.

Part of a soldier's uniform with an Australian shoulder title.
(Both photographs on this page courtesy of Oxford Archaeology on behalf of the Australian Army and the UK Ministry of Defence)

The dedication ceremony of the new Fromelles (Pheasant Wood) Military Cemetery took place in July 2010. Above, the last unknown soldier leaves Pheasant Wood, and below, his remains are carried into the new cemetery. *(Courtesy of Ian Whitlock, above, and Andrew Pittaway, below)*

The discovery of Pheasant Wood had a profound effect on Annette Darling Tebb's life (see Epilogue). Here, she is comforted by Her Excellency Governor General of Australia Quentin Bryce. *(Courtesy of Annette Darling Tebb)*

Left: The original bronze Cobbers statue (crafted by Peter Corlett) in the Australian Memorial Park near Fromelles, and (right) the replica at Melbourne's Shrine of Remembrance. Until the dedication of the latter in 2008, the name Fromelles did not appear on any memorial on Australian soil.

Tim Lycett, Sandra Playle and Lambis Englezos (left to right)
at Government House in 2010.

THE FACES OF PHEASANT WOOD

Of the 250 soldiers recovered from Pheasant Wood,
124 have been identified so far, all Australians.
Photographs have been found for 97 of the identified
soldiers and these appear on the following pages. The
search continues for photographs for the remaining 27.
The details of all the identified soldiers appear in the
appendix.

Arnott, C

Barber, W

Bennett, A

Bishop, R

Bolt, H

Bourke, H

Broadhurst, L

Brumm, N

Burney, E

Burns, R

Chinner, E

Clingan, A

Corigliano, M

Cosgriff, T

Craigie, W

Cressy, H

Croker, H

Cuckson, W

Cullen, W

Dewar, R

Dibben, E

Dunstan, B

Dyson, F

Esam, H

Farlow, S

Fenwick, R

Fletcher, F

Forland, R

Forrest, J

Francis, T

Goulding, J

Green, R

Griffiths, G

Hale, N

Harriott, L

Hepple, M

Higgins, W

Holliday, C

Holmes, A

Irvin, D

Irving, A

Jamieson, W

Jentsch, E

Johnston, C

Kendall, H

Lawlor, D

Leister, L

Livingston, D

Mayer, H

McDowell, A

McKenzie, A

McKenzie, J

McLean, H

Mendelsohn, B

Mitchell, A

Momplhait, A

Morley, J

Nevill, J

Norris, I

Pagan, G

Parker, J

Parry, F

Pflaum, R

Pheasant, W

Pitt, H

Pollard, H

Pratt, A

Pretty, W

Randall, H

Rawlings, F

Reid, M

Ridler, S

Ross, J

Russell, A

Ryan, W

Sampson, V

Scott, R

Sheridan, T

Simon, V

Spence, M

Stalgis, G

Stead, J

Steed, F

Tuck, A

Tucker, W

Turner, J

Verpillot, A

Vincent, L

Ward, C

Webb, T

Weir, A

Wildman, R

Wilkin, E

Willis, H

Wilson, E

Wilson, S

Wynn, J

branches only, as the descendant who knew the most about the soldier might not necessarily be in a matching DNA branch of the family.

Perhaps the most contentious issue we needed to address was whether or not to initiate contact with those descendants identified through our research. To pre-empt any official recovery and identification risked offering false hope and potentially causing unnecessary anguish to the families of these men. For the time being, it was ruled that other than with those descendants who approached us directly, we would not make preliminary contact, but we would reassess the decision once the government formally announced its intentions for the Pheasant Wood site.

The next stage of preparation was to build a format for conducting and storing the research. Drawing on our combined experience, we decided that first we needed to create a database for the collation of potential names and the reasons why they were included. This database was also to serve as a ready-reference for all our subsequent results and any relevant military facts about each soldier.

For the second phase of the work, a spreadsheet would provide the least troublesome method of compiling the complex details that make up individual family trees. Fortunately, Sandra had employed a similar spreadsheet on an earlier research task so already had the basic framework we required. And, even though we still needed to start from scratch with the database, I had enough experience to get the basic structure functioning within days.

The final piece of groundwork was to settle on a means

of interacting with the public and relevant authorities. It was important for us to relay our ongoing work to the community, in the hope of attracting descendants and also to serve as a point of contact for any enquiries. For this, a simple website was designed, and an attached dedicated email account went online in December 2007.

Preparations now completed, the task of probing files and scrutinising nearly century-old documentation could begin. Announcing the formation and aims of the Fromelles Descendant Database to all our local and international connections, we eagerly set out on our journey of discovering the lives and sad deaths of many young Australians – a passage to the heart of remembrance.

We began with existing lists of the Australians killed in action at Fromelles and the names of those among them who remained unaccounted for. Concentrating on the missing, we began to find clues in some files that indicated they had been buried by the Germans and therefore most probably at Pheasant Wood.

German death vouchers are small cards containing specific information taken directly from a dead soldier's identity disc discovered with his body. The vouchers appeared quite regularly in both service files and Red Cross documentation, and were a sure indication that the enemy had buried the soldier's remains. Other references, however, were a little more difficult to distinguish. We were looking also for mention of the soldier's name on a death list or the fact that his identity disc had been sent back to his family from Germany. Sometimes, the references were plain to see, but on many occasions they took the form of a single scratched notation hidden in thousands of pages of military officialdom.

Additional consideration also had to be given to those men whose last moments appeared to have been in or behind the German front line. Any man reasonably thought to have died within German-held territory, as testified to by survivors' statements to the Red Cross, had to be included on the list of those likely to have been buried by the Germans.

By the time the task of scouring the records was complete, three months later, the number of names in our list had settled at 175. With the assistance of descendants Dan Irving (1528 Private Allan Irving, 32nd Battalion) and Richard MacNeil (623 Private William Cullen, 31st Battalion), who had approached us and shared their own private research, Sandra and I discovered several others who we believed had ample justification for inclusion.

With our list now firmed up, it was time to begin preparing family trees and identifying descendants. First, we ascertained which descendants had already made themselves known to ourselves, the media or others within the Fromelles project community, as there was no need to waste precious time tracing their ancestry. Once the details of this handful of descendants had been obtained, we started work on the remaining soldiers' families. Dividing them basically into state of origin, we launched into our research.

Here is where our tried and tested system came into play.

Sandra started the ball rolling by delving into the past and pulling a family-tree structure together. Once she had established the basic framework of each family, I would then take over and bring it as far forward into the present as possible. Although plagued by the constant hindrance of privacy regulations, with some unconventional thinking and a stubborn perseverance we usually found an alternative way of breaking through the information brick wall.

It was also at about this time that we were approached by Roger Freeman, who graciously offered to assist with any work regarding the 32nd Battalion. Roger had recently published a wonderful history of the battalion, and we were keen to tap into his wealth of knowledge. In every sense, he was to become the third member of the Fromelles Descendant Database team, and his contribution was to prove invaluable to the project. Indeed, many of the 32nd Battalion men and their descendants have Roger's tireless efforts to thank for their identification.

Once the search was underway, we naturally began to learn about the lives of these men and the stories of their families. The further we probed, the more we discovered, and soon Sandra and I had to acknowledge that these soldiers were becoming more like people we knew and less like distant abstractions.

From early on, there were two soldiers from quite different backgrounds whose stories struck an immediate chord with us and exemplified the two extremes of research required to locate their families. The hunt for a descendant of one was over quite quickly and became the first of our successful searches. The hunt for the other dragged on for nearly three years.

Robert Dewar was born in London to a family with a long international maritime history. His father, also called Robert, was a very capable ship's chief engineer of forty years' experience and had been fortunate to survive the *Volturno* disaster in 1913, when a ship caught fire in the middle of a storm as it conveyed passengers – mostly immigrants – from Rotterdam to the United States. (Although several ships came to its rescue, the gale was too fierce and they were helpless to reach the stricken vessel until the sea had calmed. By then, approximately 135 people had died.)

The young Robert left England for Australia in 1907 as an unassisted immigrant and upon arrival took up a position as a tramway conductor in Sydney. Enlisting in late 1915, he embarked for Egypt just before Christmas. At the same time, Robert's father was serving on troop transports in the Mediterranean. In June 1916, a few days before Robert sailed for France, father and son had a chance encounter at Port Said. They had not seen each other for nearly nine years, and the surprise reunion may have seemed like a good omen.

It's highly likely that Robert Dewar Snr was the last parent of all the Australians killed at Fromelles to see his son alive.

On the night of 19 July, Private Robert Dewar was attached to the 55th Battalion's prisoner guard, but when the situation became desperate, he was ordered forward to support the weakening Australian line. As reinforcements for the battered 53rd Battalion, Dewar and the 55th fought hard to repel

German counter-attacks, even conducting a bayonet charge. Unfortunately, they were not able to restrain the Germans for long.

It was approaching morning when they finally realised their position was untenable and that withdrawal was the only option. As Dewar was returning to the Australian line, a shell burst close to him and, according to a witness, he was 'knocked about a lot' and killed.

Identifying Robert's descendants was astonishingly simple. A Google search of his name yielded a website about the *Volturno* disaster. At that stage, we weren't sure what we were looking at, but we were soon delighted to discover it contained a great deal of information about Robert's father and a relatively detailed biography. All we had to do then was email the website creator, who graciously forwarded our message of introduction, and in no time at all we had made contact with a living descendant in England who was more than happy to help.

It was our first search, but compared to the many searches to come it was also, unfortunately, an exception to the rule.

Born in Neuchâtel, Switzerland, in 1891, Aime Verpillot arrived in Australia via a rather circuitous route. He began his education in Switzerland but completed it in England after moving with his parents to Coventry, where his father was engaged in the watchmaking trade. After a decade in England, the family boarded ship for New Zealand in 1908, where they stayed for four years, before packing up again and sailing for Australia.

The family settled in the beachside Sydney suburb of Bondi, and Aime found employment as a metalworker fashioning scrolls for gates. So eager was he to enlist in 1915, he signed up before his naturalisation came through. In a hurried series of letters to the Department of External Affairs, he explained that he needed his naturalisation papers as quickly as possible because he was required to show them when he presented himself at Victoria Barracks: 'Having enlisted tonight I have to report at Victoria Barracks on the 6th of September 1915. I would esteem it a great favour if you would kindly return papers at your earliest convenience as I have to produce them previous to being sworn in.'

After obtaining his naturalisation papers in the nick of time, Aime served with the 53rd Battalion at Fromelles, and just days before the battle he sent a regulation army postcard home to his parents that stated simply, 'I am quite well. Letter follows at first opportunity.'

That opportunity never arrived. Very little is recorded of Aime's final moments, but, from the single surviving description of his death, it appears he was killed by a bullet early in the fight for the German front line.

Notified that their only son was missing, and later that he was presumed dead, Aime's parents were no longer content to live in the country for which he so readily gave his life and so very far from the place where he died. Immediately after hostilities ceased, they packed up their belongings and headed to war-torn France, never to set foot on Australian soil again.

That was the last trace we could find of the family, and,

despite our best efforts, it looked like the trail had gone permanently cold. Returning to this file periodically over the following three years, we had all but given up on it until a chance search through British shipping records located the passenger list containing the Verpillot family travelling from England to New Zealand.

Previously undiscovered due to a misspelling of the family's surname on the ship documentation, it provided a tantalising clue. Not only had Aime and his parents sailed to New Zealand in 1908 but it also appeared he had a sister who was travelling with them. We knew that just Aime and his parents had arrived in Australia, which meant that his sister had either died or stayed on in New Zealand.

This was typical of many of our more complex and baffling searches. It only took someone to stumble across one simple clue to unravel the entire story.

A quick check of the online New Zealand records revealed no death for Aime's sister but a marriage instead. Armed with this key piece of evidence, we only needed to make a couple of brief enquiries to finally locate Aime's niece, who had a portrait photograph of him, and, in time, to successfully identify his remains.

Chapter 9

ONE IN EVERY FAMILY

Every bullet has its billet
Some bullets more than one
For you sometimes kill a mother
When you kill a mother's son

Joseph Lee, Scottish Poet

Between 23 May and 13 June 2008, the GUARD team returned to the Pheasant Wood site again under the direction of Tony Pollard. The non-invasive testing twelve months before had established that the graves appeared intact and undisturbed. On this occasion, they were commissioned to undertake an invasive evaluation requiring limited excavation of each of the eight pits. Should they find no burials present, they would excavate the pits only to the depth necessary to ensure they were empty and to confirm that all human remains had been removed during the post-war recovery period. However, if they located human remains, they were to excavate only to a degree necessary to establish the condition of the burials and estimate the numbers

of remains present. In this case, they were also to verify nationality, evaluate identification possibilities and assess the feasibility
of recovery.

First, they marked out the approximate coordinates of each
pit by overlaying the 1916 aerial photograph that had hindered
the Allies on a current map of the site. A mechanical excavator
then dug trenches across the graves in order to pinpoint their
exact position. The excavation began by carefully removing the
layers of grass and ploughed soil and then scanning each underlying surface with metal detectors.

A number of old eyelets and buttons began to appear. These
may have been attached to groundsheets, which were commonly
used by soldiers for wrapping bodies. At a depth of approximately 25 centimetres below the present-day ground level, the
clearly defined edges of each pit emerged and then the graves
themselves, distinguished by the mottled blue and orange clay
that been used to backfill them. Taken from a level below the
subsoil when the pits were first dug in 1916, the clay was a stark
contrast to the evenness of the surrounding natural subsoil.

The evidence so far was strongly indicating that the graves
were intact and undisturbed. Had they been previously
exhumed and refilled, the sharply defined edges that ninety-
two years later still displayed original shovel marks would have
been blurry and indistinct due to over-digging. Buoyed by
these positive signs, the team reduced the excavation to metre-
square test wells known as sondages, sunk through the deposits
of each pit, allowing for preliminary investigation of their contents. Working by hand, the diggers proceeded very cautiously,

meticulously scraping away the clay and mud millimetre by millimetre. And, as each layer of soil was carefully brushed away, the past began to emerge.

On day four of GUARD's limited excavation, human remains were discovered. At first, just a tiny dirty white tip of a bone was exposed, then a joint, a finger and finally the clear outline of an entire skeletal hand. Nearby, at VC Corner Cemetery, waiting patiently among the anonymous graves of Australians recovered after the war and the memorialised names of those still missing, Lambis Englezos heard the news. After many years of campaigning against the scepticism of authorities, it was with mixed feelings that he finally achieved vindication. Relief to have found them, and sadness that these men he'd come to know so well had lain in the dirt unnoticed and unsung for so long.

In the coming days, remains were located in all of the five pits as expected, and Lambis, accompanied by fellow stalwart, friend and descendant Tim Whitford, was permitted to view them as they were uncovered. Looking at what was left of these men, Lambis and Tim believed these soldiers did not yet rest in peace and deserved a far more honourable grave. Tim later described what he saw:

> I must say that I have been given the rare honour and privilege
> to have visited those lads in the pits on multiple occasions and
> I believe that I was probably one of the last non-team members
> to have viewed the boys before backfilling. The final viewing
> had the greatest effect on me and it has definitely hardened my

resolve to advocate for exhumation, attempted identification, and reburial at a newly consecrated Pheasant Wood Cemetery. I was in two minds as to which course we must take until the final viewing and even then not until I saw the horror of pits 4 and 5. But now I know what should be done and am in earnest to achieve it . . .

. . . I have seen a handless man in a slumped sitting position with his arms still positioned above his head. He is frozen in the position he landed. One can almost imagine a German at each end of him doing the old 'one, two, three' then tossing him in. Another man is lying in a semi-fetal position with yet another man lying on top of him – this man is on his back, again with his arms extended above his head and is draped most unflatteringly across the chest of the man below him. One man still has telephone wire wrapped around his limbs which has been used to drag him into the pit. There is a man in there with a tourniquet still attached to his severed limb where some friend has vainly tried to save him.

Tim's description was validated by the results of GUARD's limited excavation. Overall, the archaeologists had unearthed approximately 16 per cent of the graves and discovered the complete or partial remains of fifty individuals entangled in layers. Displaying the telltale signs of horrendous battle wounds, the remains also testified to the vain attempts made by others to bind the awful injuries and the methods employed to ensure a swift burial. Extrapolating what they had found and applying it to the entire site, GUARD estimated the number of burials within the graves to be in keeping with the 400 mentioned in German orders, and the multitudes of badges, buttons, shrapnel and uniforms suggested a combination of both Australian and British soldiers.

For Sandra and me, the good news was that GUARD had determined the condition of the bodies to be such that they could be recovered individually and (along with the recommendation that preliminary sample testing be undertaken) concluded that DNA identification was certainly possible based on their observations.

Within days of the discovery, the trenches were backfilled and the skeletons re-entombed. A brief but touching memorial service was held at the site. Later, after the archaeologists and the observers and the media had all gone, Lambis paid a final visit to the abandoned field before heading home. Having searched for these men for so long, he was reluctant to leave them alone once more. Solemnly, he murmured, 'Don't worry, boys, I promise we'll be back for you . . . it won't be long now.' The work to find the missing men of Fromelles had finally ended, but the work to reclaim them was only just beginning.

All eyes now turned to the Australian and British governments as they deliberated about the next course of action. There was much discussion and numerous recommendations put forward by a host of commentators, descendants and historians. The general consensus was that the remains should be exhumed and reburied with honour and that all attempts be made to identify them. But there were some vocal opponents of exhumation; people who were adamant that the men should be left to lie together in peace. They argued that it was unfair for contemporary science to provide them a greater chance of identification than those recovered immediately after the war.

A first response to these protests must be the description of the graves provided by both Lambis and Tim Whitford, who made it abundantly clear that the men had not received a respectful burial. And it's simply not accurate to say they would 'unfairly benefit' from scientific advances that were not available in the 1920s. The basic concept of recovery and identification, beginning in the war years and continuing until today, has never been about employing identical processes for all but about the application of effort. Regardless of advances in science and technology, the principle applied to recovered remains of our Great War dead is to make every endeavour to identify them, utilising whatever means are available at the time. This held true immediately after the war and still applies today. To do any less would be unfair to the men who might now benefit from modern advances.

Furthermore, it would appear more than a little presumptuous to suggest the dead men would prefer to remain in the mass graves with their mates. During the war years, it was clearly apparent that the men hoped for a named headstone and respectful burial should they be killed. There can be no stronger evidence of this than their own frantic (sometimes even fatal) efforts to retrieve the bodies so that they could provide exactly that to their mates who had fallen.

Other opponents of exhumation attempted to disassociate the effects of Fromelles and the Great War by distancing them from today's society. They made bold statements that there was little or no chance of finding descendants who could remember the generation involved, let alone feel the consequences of the loss they experienced. One journalist went so far as to say it was so long ago that it just didn't matter to the families any more . . .

In recent decades, people from all walks of life have begun researching their own pasts, connecting with the places and the people that they came from. Once upon a time, it was common for Australians to want to 'cover up' their convict ancestor (if they had one). These days, he or she is more likely to be a source of patriotic pride. Cynics need only consider the phenomenal popularity of television programs such as *Find My Family* to witness how the challenges and triumphs of a distant ancestor can move and inspire their modern-day descendant. In a memorable episode of *Who Do You Think You Are?* that was screened on Australian television in 2012, the famously restrained and much-revered journalist and presenter Kerry O'Brien was seen on the verge of tears as he contemplated the terrible hardships confronting his great-great-grandfather who arrived in Australia 160 years ago. He even voiced his own surprise at his response, saying, 'I've learned that I've got more of an emotional investment in this than I thought . . .' Internet forums such as the Great War Forum and the Light Horse Forum have collectively brought together many thousands of military and family historians from across the globe, and www.ancestry.com.au is an immensely popular branch of a worldwide network of websites that boast nine million searchable family-history records.

Our experience with the Fromelles descendants proves that the naysayers' theory is without any foundation whatsoever. Many of the relatives we spoke to still keenly felt the repercussions of past despair, and there were even a few elderly ones who maintained a living contact to that generation and could identify directly with the family grief. A well-respected and high-ranking army officer (now retired) who was determinedly against the removal of the bodies has resoundingly recanted his former stance, telling us he was overwhelmed by the public response and humbled by the sensitivity and respect shown by those involved in the recovery. And, to me, there can be no greater example than Annette Darling Tebb's story at the end of this book, which vividly demonstrates the profound impact that the discovery of Pheasant Wood had on her life.

After weeks of rumours and speculation, the decision was finally announced publicly on 31 July 2008. Standing beneath the recently erected Cobbers statue at the Shrine of Remembrance in Melbourne, the Minister for Defence Science and Personnel and Minister for Veterans' Affairs, Warren Snowdon, declared to the assembled crowd that, after joint consultation with the British Government, it had been decided that an exhumation was to be undertaken and that all recovered remains were to be reburied with honour at a suitable location.

Among the audibly relieved audience members that day was Lambis Englezos. He'd promised these boys he'd be back for them and now he could be confident of fulfilling his pledge.

DNA testing was still to be formally approved, but everyone felt it would be an important part of the process. Sure enough, a few months later the DNA extraction trial was confirmed.

Up until this point, Sandra and I had been laying the foundations of our research and building upon that information. Now it was time to move into top gear. We decided to begin contacting descendants whom we had already identified and advising them of the possibility that their ancestor would be recovered.

There was always a sense of apprehension before speaking with descendants. Of course, people were often a little guarded to begin with, given the increasing prevalence of telephone and internet scams, so it was important to offer them information rather than request it. Once that rapport and trust had been established, people were almost always interested and willing to assist.

Although I was well aware of the great resurgence of interest in Australia about our First World War history, I was still pleasantly surprised to discover that only a very few had no knowledge whatsoever of their ancestor and that most knew at least something about him. The majority were fascinated by the information and thrilled that 'their soldier' might be one of those identified. Several broke down in tears as they discussed the effects the loss had on their family. For others, it was the culmination of a family search that they had privately been conducting for years.

An enormous part of our research involves the family. In many cases, we would track down a descendant, only to realise that they were not necessarily going to be an appropriate DNA candidate. This is when family knowledge kicked in. Even if our first contact didn't know much about their family tree, we found in almost every case that they knew of someone who did. Whether it was a close relative or a distant third cousin twice removed (for example), it seems that almost every family has its own 'historian' – the person who is committed by a sense of duty, curiosity or just pure pleasure to track down and collate the many tangled branches of their family line. I think of these wonderful people as the Guardians of the Family Story, and the ones we encountered in our search – Annette Darling Tebb and Tim Whitford among them – were an exceptional group.

As word spread throughout their family networks, many more descendants contacted us for information and with offers of help. It was through these unofficial networks that we were able to put together the most comprehensive gallery of photos of the men. The 2012 Fromelles Joint Identification Board brought the tally of identified men to 119, and of those we are delighted to have tracked down the photographs of 91.

Overall, the response to our work was tremendous and at times intensely emotional. Enquiries began to flood in via email and telephone, and we suddenly found ourselves completely swamped by the volume of interest. It seemed our research had come at exactly the right time. Up until now, no one had considered locating the descendants, but we had forged ahead regardless and had already produced an extensive list of family contacts that held the key to identification for many of these soldiers.

In November 2008, the Department of Defence's Australian Fromelles Project Group invited Sandra and me, as representatives of the Fromelles Descendant Database, to attend a conference at the Australian Army Headquarters in Canberra. Convened by Major General Mike O'Brien and his staff, the conference was also attended by several others with an interest in the Fromelles investigation, including Lambis and Tim Whitford, representing the Friends of the 15th Brigade; Roger Lee and Emeritus Professor Peter Dennis, representing the Army History Unit; Major General Paul Stevens of the Office of Australian War Graves; Craig Tibbetts for the Australian War Memorial; Minister for Defence Science and Personnel representative Peter Reece; Director of the National Centre for Australian Studies Professor Bruce Scates; and Jim Munro, representing the Families and Friends of the First AIF.

Once we had all introduced ourselves and outlined our respective roles in the investigation, Mike O'Brien briefly summarised the structure and aims of the Australian Fromelles Project Group. He spoke of the formation of a Fromelles Management Board comprising representatives of the French, Australian and British governments, which was designed to liaise and oversee the entire investigation. There was much discussion about the upcoming tendering process for recovery and scientific analysis. Then it was time to tackle the principal purpose of the conference: the formation of a working list of names to be released to the public.

We began by using lists compiled by Lambis and Robin Corfield, as well as an examination of soldier personnel files by Professor Peter Dennis of the Army History Unit. Every soldier's record was reviewed for plausible suggestions of him having been buried in the mass graves at Pheasant Wood. Recommendations were made for either inclusion or exclusion from the working list based on any one of the following four circumstances:

- The name of the soldier was recorded as having appeared on a German death list.
- The location of German death vouchers in a soldier's records indicated he fell at Fromelles.
- The soldier's identity disc was noted as having been returned from Germany.
- Any other evidence existed that strongly suggested the soldier died in the German trenches.

From this, a list of 175 names was compiled. Further submissions were then taken from the assembled group for consideration. Sandra and I presented examples of our work in progress to the conference and successfully recommended three additional names to the working list, bringing the total to 178.

We raised a few eyebrows among the other attendees when we put forward the contentious idea that one of those on the working list of men likely to be buried in the mass graves already had an existing named grave at Rue-Petillon Military Cemetery. This surprise discovery demanded a swift explanation lest it throw doubt over our understanding of what had occurred after the battle and negated all the work carried out so far. Fortunately, Sandra and I had done the research, and we were immediately able to explain what had happened.

At a cursory glance, there was nothing obvious to suggest that the name 1046 Private Robert Grieve Moncrieff Scott was any different from the other names included in the Department of Defence's working list of Australians thought to be buried at Pheasant Wood. However, there was an unassailable fact about his interment that set him apart from all the others. A simple search of the Australian War Memorial's Roll of Honour and the Commonwealth War Graves Commission's online database revealed that Private Robert Scott already had an identified grave in the Rue-Petillon Military Cemetery, less than 3 kilometres from Fromelles. How, then, was it possible that he could be listed as one of those thought to be buried at Pheasant Wood?

A closer inspection of his service documents at the National Archives of Australia and the Australian War Memorial's Red Cross Wounded and Missing files disclosed some intriguing intelligence that suggested an unfortunate mistake had been made. Private Robert Scott went over the top with the 32nd Battalion on 19 July 1916, but, like so many others, the circumstances regarding his death were never documented. What was known was that he was posted 'missing' after the battle until his name appeared on a German death list dated 4 November 1916, when the entry was amended to 'killed in action'. In 1917 his identity disc was returned to his family from Germany, indicating that the Germans had at one time been in possession of his body.

In 1919 a search of the Imperial Prussian War Office records in Berlin by Captain Charles Mills revealed more information about Scott. Mills had served in the 31st Battalion and was captured at Fromelles. Fluent in German, he became a liaison between the prisoners and their captors, and even befriended some of the latter. When he was released in 1917, they gave him a selection of photographs that appear today in many publications about the conflict, providing us with fascinating insights into the German point of view. He returned with the Red Cross to Germany after the war to help locate missing POWs, and in the course of his research he uncovered a number of death vouchers stating, 'The Australian Private Scott, R.G.M. No.1046, 32nd Bn, AIF, fell on 19/7/1916 in the neighbourhood of Fromelles.'

It was in this same period of time after the war that a Graves Registration Unit document attached to Scott's file indicated the recovery of what they assumed were his remains. Curiously, it also stated that a provisional cross was to be erected on the grave at Rue-Petillon Military Cemetery with the words 'Believed to be' inscribed on it. However, the most telling document was a letter written to Scott's mother in 1924 from the Imperial War Graves Commission. It explained the process by which Scott's presumed resting place could be altered from being a questionable interment into a positively identified grave: 'The cross will in due course be replaced by a permanent memorial, and should no subsequent doubt have arisen as to the identity of the grave, the words "Believed to be" can be omitted, if you wish, from the inscription on this stone.'

Understandably, Scott's grieving mother wished for her lost son to have an officially recognised grave, and she therefore agreed to this offer. From that moment on, Plot I, Row L,

Grave 46 at Rue-Petillon Military Cemetery was designated to contain the positively identified remains of 1046 Private Robert Grieve Moncrieff Scott.

What is fascinating to note from the Imperial War Graves Commission's letter is the lesser burden of proof required to determine the true identity of the grave's occupant. Apparently, it wasn't necessary to locate evidence to support the presumed identity – there only needed to be an absence of doubt. If this was the standard required for proof of identification, it was undoubtedly open to serious error and fraught with very real potential for mistakes.

And so, although Scott already had an officially marked grave, our research concluded that he qualified for the first three key elements required by the working list. It was also quite plausible to believe he may have reached the German lines, where he perished. Therefore, his inclusion on the list as having possibly been buried at Pheasant Wood was both substantiated and proper.

Once we had finally settled on the figure of 178 soldiers possibly buried by the Germans at Pheasant Wood, the conference concluded. Our objective to find the names of every one of the Australians in the mass graves had been achieved, although it was accepted that the accuracy of the list could only be proven by the success of exhumation and identification.

It is to the credit of Mike O'Brien and the Australian Fromelles Project Group that, while the working list represented the most likely candidates, they firmly maintained that any list needed to be as inclusive as possible and supported the

submission of names of any soldiers still recorded as missing
for consideration for DNA testing. The decision proved to be
extremely prudent.

Sandra and I were thrilled with private discussions at the
end of the conference when it was suggested that we might
combine our efforts with the Australian Fromelles Project
Group. The Fromelles Descendant Database research was being
recognised for its valuable contribution, and it made perfect
sense that we should come on board in a more official capacity. Regardless of what happened with this proposal, we were
assured that, in order to focus our research more efficiently,
every effort would be made to guarantee we shared our information. Valuable research time could potentially be squandered
in seeking descendants who may have already registered directly
with the Australian Fromelles Project Group. In this way, it was
important for us to know which soldiers they represented and,
if possible, the details of any descendant. Privacy was always
going to be an issue, but every effort would be made to main-
tain compliance with the law, even if it meant writing to every
known descendant for permission.

So it was to our immense disappointment that neither the
hope of official engagement nor the promised joint communication ever came to pass. Gradually, the torrent of information
between the trained professionals and the enthusiastic amateurs
reduced to a trickle, and even trying to extract the smallest piece
of harmless data seemed tantamount to breaching some kind of
state secret.

Consequently, our research began to consume a great many

additional hours, and this, combined with the need for considerable personal funding, began to affect progress. We requested
a small grant from the Army History Unit to help us complete
the project, and we were turned down flat on the basis that they
did not fund 'volunteers'. Disheartened by rejection and forced
to re-evaluate where we were taking the research, Sandra and I
were still fiercely committed to identifying the boys at Pheasant
Wood and pushed on with the work, albeit at a more personally
sustainable pace.

However, the gods of bureaucracy hadn't finished with us
yet. It was with much dismay that we discovered in March 2010
that a substantial chunk of research had been lifted directly
from our website and published in a Department of Defence
document released to both the media and public. Comprising
a large number of photographs that had taken us a great deal of
time and effort to trace and compile, the release contained no
acknowledgement of the source in its contents. The suggestion
to anyone who read it was that the research had been conducted
by the Australian Fromelles Project Group.

At this point, I allowed my pride to step in, and I loudly
voiced my disapproval at what I perceived to be unethi-
cal behaviour. As the founder of the Fromelles Descendant
Database, I was well aware of the generous assistance freely
given to our project by volunteers from around the globe, and
to see their efforts unfairly attributed to others was just too
bitter a pill to swallow. I remonstrated with the minister for veterans' affairs and defence personnel, Alan Griffin, via protracted
correspondence. Although he did not offer a direct apology,

he did eventually admit to the Department of Defence's inadvertent use of our research and failure to properly acknowledge its source. He went on to assert that the document in question had been completely removed from the department's website. Although this was true in terms of there no longer being any direct link to it on their website, the document remained freely accessible to anyone with a mind to find and download it.

Emerging somewhat battered and more than a little wary, we felt nonetheless that our point had been made and there was no longer any need to pursue it further. Casting aside our disappointment, we considered the overall investigation and had to recognise that, despite our private frustrations, the members of the Australian Fromelles Project Group appeared as sincerely dedicated to their task as we were to ours. With far more at stake than personal pride, we accepted that any lingering bitterness would only be detrimental to the combined input of both camps and the ongoing process of identification. Sandra and I therefore resolved to put the entire unfortunate chapter behind us and continue moving forward with our work.

Three months after the conference, the attendees all received an email from Mike O'Brien informing us that the working list of 178 names, with the addition of thirteen more, would soon be released to the public. This was the first we had heard of the extra thirteen names, and, after examining their files, we were perplexed by their inclusion because the historical criteria that had been employed so effectively was entirely absent in some of the cases.

Mike advised us that the thirteen had been provided by the department's official researcher, who had been ensconced in the

Red Cross Archives in Geneva, Switzerland. He explained that while the researcher had not located the actual German death lists, he had discovered records substantiating the possibility that these men were also buried at Pheasant Wood.

It turns out that this 'discovery' was far beyond just a few forgotten documents. In 2008 Professor Peter Barton, eminent historian, author and co-secretary of the British All Party Parliamentary War Graves and Battlefield Heritage Group, was commissioned by the Australian authorities to conduct a search of the Bavarian state records and International Red Cross Archives for documents related to the Fromelles burials.

We were well aware that the Germans notified the Allies about prisoners, deaths and burials by means of documentation forwarded from the International Red Cross in neutral Switzerland. Although Peter hadn't yet found the coveted death lists, he had apparently discovered a host of other references suggesting these thirteen men had been buried by the Germans after the battle. This was great news for the Fromelles team. It was only later that we learned the breathtaking scale of Peter's discovery and the Aladdin's cave of information he had uncovered, which went far beyond the Fromelles investigation.

Peter was one of the first historians to request access to the International Red Cross Archives in Geneva. His access granted, in early 2009 he walked into a basement that was lined floor to ceiling with dusty, dilapidated records virtually untouched since the armistice in 1918. He began examining the boxes and soon realised that he had stumbled upon one of the most significant historical finds related to the 1914–18 conflict.

Estimated to contain records of over twenty million soldiers, the mountain of card indexes and ledgers listed precise details of names, ranks, nationalities, dates, times and exact burial locations of literally tens of thousands of men. It was an astonishing find, with far-reaching historical value. The United Nations Educational, Scientific and Cultural Organisation (UNESCO) considers the archive akin to a World Heritage Site, and it has incorporated it into its Memory of the World program.

The potential of this collection to reveal the whereabouts of individuals whose remains were unfound or identify those lying in graves inscribed only as 'Known Unto God' is mind-boggling. And so to the question on everyone's lips: why were these invaluable records not accessed before? The staggeringly simple response from the International Red Cross was . . . no one asked!

Chapter 10

MARKING TIME

You live as long as you are remembered.

Russian proverb

It was now a proven reality that the lost soldiers of Fromelles lay undisturbed in the mass graves at Pheasant Wood, and the Commonwealth War Graves Commission was asked by the Australian and British governments to administer their recovery and reburial. In addition, the Commission was charged with the responsibility of providing a suitable place for the men to be honourably interred.

Although remains of Great War soldiers are uncovered in France and Belgium on a reasonably regular basis, the recovery of hundreds of bodies at Pheasant Wood was extraordinary, and accommodating such numbers required a great deal of deliberation. In the end, it was agreed to construct the first new

Commonwealth War Graves Commission cemetery in over fifty years: the Fromelles (Pheasant Wood) Military Cemetery.

An elderly local lady, Marie-Paul Demassiet, was the owner of the property where the burial pits were located, and she kindly agreed to donate the land. At first, it appeared to be the obvious choice for the cemetery, but, due to constant ground water, flooding issues and access problems, it was ruled unfit for the purpose. A new site about 330 metres south-west from the mass graves was identified as the most suitable location. It was situated adjacent to the road that leads north past the Australian Memorial Park, with its distinctive bronze Cobbers statue (crafted by Peter Corlett), and the VC Corner Cemetery. The spire of Fromelles' Saint Jean Baptiste church would overlook the new cemetery from across the street.

The new Fromelles (Pheasant Wood) Military Cemetery was designed with many traditional elements of Commonwealth War Graves cemeteries in mind. It forms a distinctive hexagonal shape, partly to conform to site boundaries but also to produce a radial layout of graves all focused towards the Cross of Sacrifice on its terrace at the southern end, from where the viewer can catch glimpses across the former battlefield. Although the test pit excavation in 2008 proved that only five of the eight mass graves contained significant numbers of remains, based on GUARD's initial maximum estimates and similar numbers suggested in the orders of Major General Julius von Braun when constructing the mass graves in 1916, the new cemetery was planned to accommodate 400 graves, and its construction was to run parallel with the recovery operation in preparation for respectful interment of remains at the earliest opportunity.

The tenders for the final phase of the recovery work were assessed during two separate evaluations. The first stage called for expressions of interest from professional organisations and requested an estimate of costs for the project. In November 2008 three companies responded and lodged expressions of interest: GUARD, Oxford Archaeology and Birmingham University. Based on these submissions, all three were then invited to tender for the contract of managing all archaeological services for the recovery. It was envisaged that the contract would encompass the entire process. In addition to details of the actual excavation and recovery, the companies had to submit information regarding all proposed analysis of recovered remains and associated artefacts by employing appropriate forensic methods as well as site-management strategies addressing concerns about the effects of ground water and weather.

The three tenders were evaluated for merit, ability, technical superiority and financial value. The assessment recommendation was then put before the Fromelles Management Board – a panel formed as a result of the Pheasant Wood discovery and co-chaired by members of the British Ministry of Defence and Australian Defence Force representing their respective governments. On 25 February 2009, it was announced that the contract had been awarded to Oxford Archaeology.

Oxford Archaeology is one of the largest independent archaeological and heritage organisations in Europe, with permanent offices in Britain and France. Since its formation in 1973, it has grown in size and reputation, and today carries out substantial commercial archaeological fieldwork across Europe. The company employs approximately 350 people, including burial archaeologists, heritage-management and finds specialists. Even so, its appointment stirred up some controversy among certain Fromelles research groups, as many had felt sure, given their prior association and knowledge of the site, that GUARD would be re-engaged for the final work. Nevertheless, preparations for the excavation forged ahead.

A similar tender process was launched to determine which company offered the best DNA profiling program. Five companies were approached but only two responded. After a period of formal evaluation, the announcement was made that LGC Forensics had been awarded the contract.

To be implemented over two stages, the DNA analysis would begin with pilot testing on samples from the graves. The soil at Pheasant Wood is predominantly made up of a fine-grained clay that is largely impermeable to moisture. The graves that were more loosely packed with bodies allowed moisture to run back in, creating a waterlogged environment that was more favourable to DNA preservation. The spade edges of the pit then made a barrier to further water movement. In addition, the slight slope of the site led to the frequent occurrence of standing water. For those pits that lay along the southern edge of the woodland, preservation was uniformly poorer because the nearby trees and plants leached moisture from the soil.

And then there were random factors such as the amount of chloride of lime that the Germans had added at every layer in each pit to promote decomposition. Those bodies that were wrapped in groundsheets had decomposed at a slower rate, and the presence of metal artefacts scattered through the pits increased the acidity of the soil.

Bearing in mind that the remains had been in different graves for over ninety years and that those graves were in very different conditions, this evaluation was needed to establish whether DNA was likely to be extracted from the remains, and, if so, whether it was viable for profiling. Should the pilot test reveal quantity and quality of DNA sampling, then a full analysis program would take place.

Assembling a team of thirty specialists headed by Dr Louise Loe, Oxford Archaeology established three distinct operations within the Pheasant Wood excavation site. The field team conducted the work of excavation and recovery, and comprised archaeologists experienced in identification of human remains, surveyors using digital technology to precisely record the location of remains and items found within the graves, and a finds specialist responsible for the recovery, recording and conservation of all items located.

The laboratory team worked from a nearby compound, made up of a series of purpose-built portable cabins housing scientific laboratories and a mortuary. Here, the forensic pathologist, anthropologists, radiographer and mortuary technologist could examine and process the remains prior to storage and assist DNA specialists by obtaining relevant samples.

The final team consisted of the educational liaison members. Their role was to provide regular progress updates to relevant government departments and supply material useful for public releases.

In addition to the Oxford Archaeology on-site specialists, the Fromelles Management Board also appointed two highly experienced subject-matter experts, Professor Margaret Cox and Dr Peter Jones, to support and advise them in relation to forensic anthropology and DNA analysis respectively.

Excavation of the Pheasant Wood mass graves commenced in early May 2009 after a brief sod-turning ceremony. Proceeding cautiously, to decrease the likelihood of striking disaster in the form of a discarded Great War artillery shell or mortar, mechanical excavators began to strip away the topsoil to a depth of about 20 centimetres. Once the original pits dug by GUARD in 2008 had been re-excavated, the Oxford archaeologists, dressed in full personal-protection equipment, moved outwards towards the edges of each grave. As the layers of thick sticky clay were methodically removed, the skeletal remains of the men revealed themselves.

Great care had to be taken from this point on. It was immensely important that all remains and artefacts were recorded in their exact locations to assist in the future identification process. If an object was moved away from its position without being recorded, it could risk being disassociated from a particular set of remains. If that item subsequently provided evidence of a name, then the fundamental role it might have played in terms of identification may well have been lost.

Leaving no clod of earth unchecked, the archaeologists progressed through the layers of bodies. For much of the time, they had to sprawl awkwardly on timber planks spanning the width of the graves. As remains and artefacts were lifted out, they were immediately conveyed to the on-site laboratories for recording, processing, analysis, preservation and, finally, storing. The 'chain of custody' for each item was strictly observed to ensure a clear record of its location at any given time.

Apart from brief delays when ground water seeped into the open graves during periods of rain, the recovery operation moved briskly. After seventeen weeks, all eight of the graves had been excavated. Five of the graves each held in the vicinity of fifty men, while, of the remaining three, one contained the remains of three men and the other two were empty, as expected. In total, 250 sets of remains were recovered from the mass graves. In time, it was tentatively determined that about 200 were Australian soldiers, three were probably British soldiers and the remainder were yet to be attributed a nationality.

Multitudes of artefacts were recovered with the bodies, which offered a fascinating glimpse into a soldier's war. Aside from the expected buttons, buckles, badges and uniform fragments, the more personal items instantly distinguished these men as individuals and provided a heightened sense of poignancy to their very human stories. It was common practice for soldiers to fashion jewellery and other items from the remnants of shell casings, and a few pieces of this 'trench art' were recovered, including rings probably intended for a loved one back home. A variety of religious items, such as crucifixes, saints' medallions and rosaries, were unearthed, and even an exceptionally well preserved bible was found, with passages still visibly underlined. A leather coin purse came to light containing a number of coins, including eight of Ottoman Turkish currency, indicating that the soldier could well have fought at Gallipoli. Several pipes were recovered, as was a brass petrol cigarette lighter.

Perhaps the most evocative item was a small piece of thick paper folded up inside a gas-mask hood. It had to be dried before it could be examined, but when the scrap was finally unfolded it revealed itself to be a second-class return-journey train ticket from Fremantle to Perth in Western Australia. Although it's easy to presume the ticket belonged to one of the Western Australians buried at Pheasant Wood, it must be remembered that the port of Fremantle was also a regular stopover for troopships sailing to war from other states of Australia and the ticket may have been purchased by one of those men on shore leave. Regardless of who the owner was, there can be no doubt that he was Australian and had probably kept this ticket as a memento of his last moments on home soil. He may even have considered it a good-luck charm, to be used on his return.

While the recovery operation was still in full swing, everyone eagerly awaited the results of the pilot DNA testing. Samples of teeth, small bones and long bones had been taken from different parts of the two graves being assessed to represent both the most promising and least favourable samples in terms of potential DNA extraction. An exclusion zone was erected around every grave, and the archaeologists removed the samples as quickly as possible once the soil had been brushed away. The samples were then immediately placed in cold storage, logged and bar-coded before being transported to LGC Forensics' laboratories, where the testing occurred.

On 10 August 2009, exactly one month before the recovery operation was complete, the Australian and British governments jointly announced the results of the DNA pilot study. LGC Forensics concluded that there was a uniform degree of preservation throughout the graves and that, from all the samples tested, teeth appeared to be producing the highest quality and quantity of DNA. This is often the case with digs of this nature, with teeth holding the best genetic material, followed by long bones and then short bones. Using a number of steps and procedures, profiles for both paternal (Y marker) and maternal (mitochondrial or X marker) DNA had been sequenced from the samples, and, although admittedly degraded over time and by the conditions, they yielded results that would be eminently useable for matching purposes.

Based on these findings, the governments of both countries agreed that a full program of DNA analysis should be implemented. All sets of remains and known descendants who were willing and who fitted the required criteria of paternal or maternal descent would be tested. If the Fromelles soldier had children, the direct lineage could only be established through the Y marker passed to his male descendants. There would be no mitochondrial marker in his daughters, as they would have inherited it from their mother. But, as many of the Fromelles men were still very young themselves and had no children, direct lineage would have to be established by either the soldier's brother's male descendants (as all would have inherited the same Y marker from the soldier's father), or alternatively via his sister's male and female descendants (who would have inherited their mitochondrial markers from the soldier's mother). Finally, if the soldier had no siblings, direct lineage could be determined either through his uncle's male descendants or his aunt's male and female descendants, as they shared their markers with the soldier's paternal grandfather and maternal grandmother respectively.

While the physical work of archaeologists and anthropologists began to wind down, the labours of genealogists moved to centre stage. Sandra and I had already begun locating descendants but held off from initiating contact until the DNA process was confirmed to go ahead. By the time the announcement was made, we had accumulated a partial database of names that could be acted upon immediately.

First, we had to contact the people we had identified as descendants so that we could verify our results and tie up the loose ends relating to lines of descent where we had struck brick walls. Then we handed over the list of gathered names to the Department of Defence's Fromelles Project Group. It was their job to do the follow-up. Our research continued, but from this point on it was decided that once contact had been made with the descendants, we would direct them to register with the Fromelles Project Group and they would take it from there.

In building its database, the Fromelles Project Group relied on those people who directly contacted them and did not actively seek descendants through research, though the information we provided for them would almost certainly have been included in their lists.

In retrospect, I must admit it was a little disappointing to us that, apart from the occasional message of thanks, our work was never acknowledged in any formal way. Of course, public recognition was the last thing on our minds when we took on the Fromelles Descendant Database project, but admittedly it remains somewhat frustrating that our 'amateur' ranking automatically relegated our considerable achievements to obscurity. The fact that so many non-professionals were involved in the discovery and recovery of the Fromelles soldiers is something that we should be celebrating. After all, if it wasn't for a humble school teacher who decided to follow up on a hunch, the men would still be lost to us, tangled in rough burial pits at the edge of a lonely wood.

Chapter 11

EUREKA MOMENTS

When you remember me, it means that you have carried something of who I am with you, that I have left some mark of who I am on who you are. It means that you can summon me back to your mind even though countless years and miles may stand between us.

Frederick Buechner, writer and theologian

The search for descendants of the men believed buried at Pheasant Wood was complex and often disheartening. Yet it was the unravelling of the most difficult cases that yielded the most surprising results and with them the greatest satisfaction.

The case of 1130 Private James Gordon has already been introduced in Chapter 1 – a simple enough scenario of enterprising young brothers who got away with the common ruse of enlisting while they were underage. However, we had no clue about their double deceptions when we set out to track the descendants of one of our missing soldiers, and we confronted many dead ends before we finally stumbled upon the right path.

To begin with, Sandra began working on the family tree

using birth, death and marriage records. These precious certificates provide crucial information, and once they have been
applied for they can take anything from a few minutes to download on the computer to several weeks to arrive by post. Much
depends on the office where the application is lodged and the
state of their records for the relevant period of time.

Fortunately, James's birth certificate was easy to locate, and
Sandra established that he was born in Carlton, Melbourne,
in 1903 to parents William Gordon and Ellen Eliza Lewis.
However, alarm bells rang immediately because he was far too
young to have served during the Great War (enlistment age was
eighteen and he would have been about thirteen!). A detailed
investigation ensued as a result of this peculiarity and we eventually discovered that James Gordon had in fact died in 1905,
when he was less than two years old.

I began to explore the military records, and a closer
inspection of James's service file provided a necessary clue. It
contained two pension applications submitted by his mother,
Ellen, who stated the soldier to be 'Gordon, John (enlisted as
James Gordon)'. Returning to the birth indexes, Sandra con-
firmed that the infant James Gordon did indeed have two older
brothers. The first, William Lewis Gordon, was born in South
Australia in 1899 and the second, John Gordon, was born in
Carlton, Melbourne, in 1900. In addition, there was a sister,
Ethel, who was born in Carlton in 1906.

These dates still meant that Private Gordon was underage,
but they seemed more plausible. On the downside, we couldn't
find decisive proof that indicated which one of the older

brothers had enlisted, and the further we looked the more con-
fusing the issue became.

I began a thorough check of the National Archives of
Australia and turned up three relevant service records. The first
was for 'William Lewis Gordon', who enlisted in 1915, but
somehow his real age was discovered and he was sent home. The
second was for 'John Gordon', who enlisted in July 1915 and
was accepted into the 2nd Divisional Signal Company, where
he served throughout the war. Significantly, this soldier gave his
birthplace on the attestation paper as Port Adelaide, suggesting he was the eldest brother, William. Because he had failed to
enlist the first time using his own name, he had then tried and
succeeded in enlisting using his younger brother's name.

The final record was for 'James Gordon', who also enlisted
in July 1915. His birthplace was given as Carlton, so we were
confident that we had found the real John Gordon. It appeared
that these determined young brothers had swapped names
around between themselves and their deceased infant brother in
an effort to fool the enlistment board.

But the complications didn't stop there.

Sandra was focusing on the family tree of the boys' mother,
Ellen, hoping to find clues to a possible descendant. Poring
through Victorian cemetery records, she located the monumental compartment of Ellen Gordon at Springvale Necropolis
in Melbourne. She was buried with her infant son James and
her middle-aged son William, who had died in 1950. This
left John as the only possible family member to have died at
Fromelles.

To our enormous relief, we believed we had found the proof we needed, but a final check of the Victorian Death Index threw our research into turmoil once more. In 1950, the index only had a listing for John Gordon. We now had the same year of death for both brothers. Could this mean that neither of them had actually enlisted and that Private James Gordon was in fact someone else entirely? The only other possible conclusion was that both the 1950 cemetery record and death index referred to the same man but that one of the names was incorrect.

Our next step was to obtain copies of the death certificates and examine them more closely. When they arrived several weeks later, things began to fall into place. As we'd suspected, the dates of death for both William and John were identical, and it appeared there had been an error. The certificate attributed to John had been prepared by the coroner, because the death had taken place in a psychiatric hospital, but it also provided the final proof of identity of the soldier who lay at Pheasant Wood. The age given on the certificate indicated the deceased was born in 1899 and began his life in South Australia. Clearly, the 1950 death certificate was referring to William, and thus the cemetery inscription, endorsed by his sister, Ethel, was correct.

We can't confirm how the mistake was made, but it is probably because William had served using the name John Gordon and, for the purpose of obtaining repatriation benefits, he registered himself using the same name.

Now we had our proof. 1130 Private James Gordon was in reality his brother John – as originally indicated by the pension records in the service file.

John was born on 18 September 1900, so at the time of his death, he was only fifteen years, ten months and one day old. We were well aware of a younger Australian soldier named Jim Martin who had succumbed to disease on a hospital ship during the Gallipoli campaign, but we wondered whether there had been a younger soldier actually killed in action.

To begin with, our search produced only one possible candidate: 2251 Private John Auguste Emile Harris of the 2nd Battalion. In Harris's service record, his father stated he had only been fifteen years and ten months old when killed at Gallipoli on 8 August 1915. We located a record of his birth in 1899, but it wasn't for several weeks until a precise date could be obtained. Harris was born on 6 October 1899, making him fifteen years, ten months and two days old when he was severely injured during the legendary charge at Lone Pine and died soon after. One day older than John Gordon.

For some years, we believed that we had unearthed the youngest known Australian soldier ever to be killed in action. But, in April 2011, the true age of 5071 Private Leslie Thomas Prior of the 23rd Battalion was discovered when one of his descendants decided to do some research after his mother told him her great-step-uncle was only fourteen years old when he enlisted. Coincidentally, Prior was also born in Carlton, but he had been seven months younger than John Gordon when he was killed and his body lost at the second battle of Bullecourt in May 1917.

Regardless of which lad was the youngest to die, the loss of so many Australian boys just like Martin, Harris, Gordon and

Prior was truly lamentable and signifies the gaping generational hole left in Australian society by the Great War.

If uncovering the truth of John's identity had been difficult, locating his descendants was to prove almost impossible. Sandra established that his older brother, William, died unmarried and childless at the age of fifty-one at the Mont Park Hospital for Mental Hygiene in Victoria. In the 1924 Australian Electoral Rolls, he was listed as 'John Gordon – Traveller', living with his parents. Then, in 1943, he was known as 'William Gordon – Unemployed', living with his sister, Ethel, in Fitzroy.

When he was admitted to Mont Park, he was suffering from pneumonia, and it was cardiac failure that eventually caused his untimely demise. We can only speculate as to what brought William to Mont Park in the first place as, owing to privacy laws, almost all mental-health records have been closed since the early 1900s. However, it is reasonable to assume that, like so many other men, his war experiences played a significant part in his mental breakdown. He may also have harboured a nagging sense of guilt throughout his adult life for enticing his younger brother to enlist in the deadly conflict that stole his life.

John's only other direct sibling was his younger sister, Ethel. Although she lived a relatively long life, when she died in 1973 she had never married or had children, so the direct line of John's branch of the family ended with his generation. If we were to find descendants, we would need to cast our net much wider.

At the outset, we attempted to make headway along the Gordon branch of the family, but there was scant information about John's father, who had emigrated from Scotland, and it was exceptionally difficult to pinpoint which Gordon family was the correct one because it was such a common name at the time. Guessing was not an option. We needed to be confident of our family links, so we turned our attention to the Lewis side of his family.

Fortunately, John's mother hailed from a South Australian pioneering family, and it didn't take long to identify his aunts and uncles in the Lewis line. Yet, every time we ventured down these branches, we encountered seemingly insurmountable blocks. Children had died either young or unmarried, or had no recorded offspring of their own. For more than eighteen months, we returned again and again to John Gordon's family, and, apart from a few minor advances, we had no tangible success.

Then, late in 2010, a chance discovery resulting from a random search through newspaper archives provided the break-through we needed. We'd found nothing closer to home, so I decided to look through the *West Australian* newspapers even though there was no tangible link to the area. A marriage announcement dated 1947 indicated that a single branch of the Lewis family had moved west from South Australia. This time, I was able to trace the family using electoral rolls and telephone records, and within two days had made contact with the family of John Gordon's cousin. She in turn put me in touch with another two descendants, and suddenly we were very much back in business.

After such a challenging search, we'd hoped for a swift and satisfying ending to the James Gordon story, but unfortunately this was not to be. The family members eagerly contacted the organisation that had succeeded the Fromelles Project Group, namely the Unrecovered War Casualties Office (UWC), fully expecting to provide DNA samples for testing. It was nearly eighteen months and several reminders (from myself included) later that the UWC finally got back to the Gordon descendants and began the process for identification. No reason was given for the delay, and I hope it was merely an aberration, though I have heard of inexplicably lengthy waits for other descendants.

Our fingers are crossed that, in future rounds of DNA testing, the young lad from Carlton will finally be identified and recognised for his sacrifice.

The investigation to locate descendants of 4840 Private Leslie Leister is possibly the greatest challenge we have faced so far.

Serving with the 55th Battalion, Leister had last been seen by Private Barker lying wounded in a dugout in the German lines:

> *He was wounded at Fleurbaix on July 19th. He got over past the German front line and was wounded there in the hip. He was put in a dug out in the German front line. I saw him there. He was lying on what looked like a stretcher. He seemed quite cheerful and pretty right but could not move much. That is the last I know of him.*

Leslie's service record told us that he was born in about 1894 but adopted as a child into the family of his aunt and uncle,

Robert and Eliza Leister, at Parkes, New South Wales. Given the common surname, we initially believed he must have been the direct blood relative of his uncle's family. However, a closer examination of his file revealed a letter from the Mutual Life and Citizens Assurance Company stating that he was also known as 'Jack Walsh'.

This piece of information meant that we could no longer assume he was directly related to his uncle, as he had been given a new name when adopted. Therefore, it became necessary to explore the family links of both his adoptive parents to try to establish his true parentage. Bafflingly, there was no sign of a Walsh on either side.

It was at this point that fate stepped in and provided a key piece to the puzzle. Quite coincidentally, a friend and fellow member of the Families and Friends of the First AIF, Graeme Hosken, had recently been to Parkes and on the spur of the moment decided to photograph headstones related to the Great War in the local cemetery. One of these headstones included a memorial to Leslie Leister and was on the grave of John and Sarah Way. The wording on the headstone quite clearly showed that Leslie had been the grandson of this couple and therefore the child of one of their daughters. This immediately focused our attention on the sisters of Leslie's adoptive mother, Eliza Leister, whose maiden name was Way and who was one of the daughters of John and Sarah.

Upon examining Eliza's family, it became apparent that her sister, Sarah Jane Way, was most likely to be Leslie's mother, as records indicated she had died only a couple of years after he was born. The problem we had already discovered was that she had not married a man called Walsh. Records indicated that Sarah had been married twice: the first time in 1882 to Robert Whiteman, who had died in 1884, and a second time in 1894 to John Young. Both couples had children during the period of their marriages but it did not appear likely that Leslie Leister was among their offspring.

Stumped yet again, we decided to throw the search wide open. We looked through births for all babies called Jack Walsh and turned up nothing. The next step was what we call a 'wild-card' search through the New South Wales birth register of all Jack Ws in the 1890s. It was a formidable task, but after many hours of diligently trawling these records we discovered the birth in 1894 of Jack W. Whiteman at Parkes to mother Sarah Jane. It was then the penny finally dropped.

After losing her husband in 1884, Sarah Jane Whiteman (as she was then known) gave birth to an illegitimate child before her second marriage ten years later. As governed by the laws of the time, the child was required to take his mother's legal sur-name, which was Whiteman. However, as often occurred, the child's middle name would reflect the surname of the biological father, and in this case we hoped that the 'W' would stand for 'Walsh'.

Jack Whiteman's birth certificate arrived weeks later, and our patience was rewarded. In 1894, the birth name was offi-cially recorded as Jack Walsh Whiteman.

Armed with this vital piece of information, we began to trace the families of Leslie's newly discovered half-siblings and within days had located and contacted a number of their descendants. From what they were able to tell us, it transpired that after the death of Sarah Jane in 1898, their respective blood relatives raised the children of both her marriages. Although the siblings maintained a close relationship, none of them ever realised that Leslie Leister was in fact their half-brother.

Looking back on this case, only now can we appreciate the extraordinary achievement we had made through sustained effort and lateral thinking. With nothing more than an adoptive name as a starting point, we had uncovered the truth of Leslie Leister's illegitimate birth, identified his true parentage, established his birth name and located his descendants.

A sad postscript to this investigation occurred in August 2010 when over a hundred headstones at Parkes Cemetery were smashed in a callous act of pointless vandalism. Having finally been identified as a place where Leslie's family could grieve his loss nearly a century after his death, the Way headstone now lies shattered beyond repair.

A friendly face with head tilted slightly to one side suggests a light-hearted personality open to all kinds of fun. The pipe is jauntily set between smiling lips, and kindly eyes hint at a gentle nature. But there is something more if you take the time to really gaze at the tinted photograph: an air of uneasiness. It isn't the unfamiliar military uniform and nor is it the swagger stick held awkwardly in his hands. Belying his convivial features is a distinct sense of sadness borne from years of adversity. The photo-graph is more than just an image of an Australian soldier; it's of a young man who has suffered much hardship and loss in his relatively short life.

It was a bittersweet day in 1883 when Mary McGee gave birth to her first child, John (Jack) Thomas Joyce, in Wolverhampton, England. She had married Thomas Joyce in 1874, and it had taken nine long years for a baby to arrive, but sadly her husband was not there to share the joy. Thomas's death certificate reveals he died only weeks before his son emerged into the world.

A year later, Mary met and married John Rose at Cannock, Staffordshire, and later bore the first of Jack's half-siblings, Robert and Ellen. Then, in about 1892, John and Mary Rose moved to the colliery town of Cambois, Northumberland, taking the three children with them. They set up home amid the drab streets of post-Industrial Revolution miners' cottages, where John immediately set to work at the local mine as a hewer. Here, John and Mary had their last two children, Mary and Edwin.

By 1901 both Jack Joyce and his half-brother Robert Rose were also employed at the colliery, as underground mine workers. Although this meant three incomes for the family, the lives of colliery workers involved long hours and relentless hard toil. No doubt, the strain took its toll on Mary and hastened her untimely death in 1909.

That same year, Jack decided to leave England and seek his fortune in Australia. He landed at Fremantle, Western Australia, but chose not to hunt for employment in his previous trade.

With the memory of the confined and fetid conditions of English coal mines still all too vivid, being never more than a spark or choking breath from death, he shied away from the dark underground existence and instead pursued a life of fresh air and boundless horizons as a drover.

He settled near Wagin, a thriving sheep-farming area southeast of Perth. It was there that Jack became acquainted with local nurse Rita Tourney, and a strong bond developed between them. Whether the bond may have deepened into something else, we'll never know, as the Great War intervened. The Anzac landing at Gallipoli and glowing newspaper articles extolling Australia's feats of arms seduced many young men with the promise of adventure and battlefield glory, Jack Joyce among them. In a gesture of commitment to Rita, he named her as his next of kin and requested all his worldly possessions be left to her in the event of his death.

Our search for the family of Jack Joyce began in Cambois, but, even with the assistance of several local family-history groups and Northumberland historical societies, we made little headway. We were able to locate Jack and the Rose family on the British 1891 census at Cambois, and, in 1911, after Jack had sailed for Australia, the Roses were found to be living in Morpeth. By this time, Jack's half-sister, Ellen Rose, was married to John Beddow but she died giving birth to their second child. Fortunately, Ellen and John already had a daughter, Mary Hannah Beddow, so hope of finding a maternally linked descendant persisted. We established that Mary Beddow married Frederick Troup and identified the names of the two children born of their union. Then a check of the death indexes revealed that both died in infancy, and with these children ended any hope we had of finding a descendant along that particular line of Jack's family.

Returning to the other Rose children, only Mary offered a direct maternal line, but the trail petered out almost immediately. We managed to discover the marriage of a woman named Mary Rose but there was not a strong enough link to the family and, even if we could confirm it, there was no record of children from the union. It seemed that the Rose family was not going to provide us with the descendants we needed. With hindsight, this may not have been what Jack wanted anyway.

Disheartened, we decided to try to track down the only known link to Jack in Australia. Although not a relative, Rita Tourney had obviously meant a great deal to Jack, and we wondered whether she might have kept any mementos of their friendship. It wasn't hard to piece together what became of Rita in the years after the war. She married a returned light horseman named Alex Calder and they had two daughters, one of whom we discovered lived just down the road from Sandra. An introductory phone call led to a revelatory meeting with Rita's daughter Yvonne.

Rita had passed away some years before, but we learned from Yvonne that she never forgot Jack. After the war, Rita applied to the Army Base Records for Jack's medals on the basis that she was recorded as his next of kin. It was her understanding, as Jack told her all those years ago, that he had no family whatsoever. We now know this is not quite the truth, but it does perhaps suggest that Jack never felt the Roses to be his family and that, after his mother's death, there was nothing keeping him in England.

Once he'd arrived in Australia, he either lost touch or purposely abandoned contact with his former family. This had unfortunate repercussions, because even though Jack nominated Rita for his next of kin, her application for his medals was denied on the basis that she was not a blood relative. As Jack left no clues about his blood kin, his medals were never issued and remain unclaimed to this day.

Yvonne then produced a precious relic of Rita's devoted friendship to Jack: an old sepia-tinted photograph of Jack that she had faithfully kept all those years. Dressed in his smart new uniform, he posed for a portrait in front of a row of tents at Blackboy Hill training camp on the eastern outskirts of Perth, and he'd given it to Rita as a keepsake. It is the only known image we have of Jack Joyce.

Chapter 12

A QUESTION OF BURIAL

When war shall cease this lonely unknown spot
Of many a pilgrimage will be the end,
And flowers will shine in this now barren plot
And fame upon it through the years descend:
But many a heart upon each simple cross
Will hang the grief, the memory of its loss.

**Excerpt from 'A Soldier Cemetery' by Sergeant John William Streets,
York and Lancaster Regiment, killed in action 1 July 1916**

The startling revelation that Robert Grieve Moncrieff Scott was already named on a grave at Rue-Petillon Cemetery was the impetus behind our research taking an entirely different direction. Because the number of Australians recovered from the mass graves was much higher than those named on the initial Department of Defence list, it became apparent that we needed to try to identify each and every one of them. We couldn't assume that the Germans had located identity discs or other forms of identification on every single body they buried at Pheasant Wood.

The task of interring hundreds of bodies – many of them with ghastly wounds and in the early stages of putrefaction – would not have been something they lingered over.

The chaos of battle would have destroyed the means of identifying many bodies, and others may have had their belongings removed by their comrades before they fell into German hands. It follows that if the German gravediggers were unable to gather identification from certain bodies, they would have no idea who they were and their names would not have been included on the prepared death lists later forwarded to the Red Cross.

Until the final recovery, researchers expected that the identity of these men would almost exclusively be found among the files of the missing. Nobody had ever thought to check the records of those with existing identified graves. However, the implications of an error made in Scott's case begged the question whether any similar mistakes had been committed. With this in mind, the Fromelles Descendant Database team embarked on a meticulous search through the files of each Australian with an existing named grave who had been killed at Fromelles. Using the precedent set by the Scott case, we uncovered a further four men with recorded graves who appeared likely to have been buried at Pheasant Wood.

715 LANCE CORPORAL RALPH JOHNSON, 31ST BATTALION

Born in 1897 in Healesville, Victoria, to parents Hubert and Alice, Ralph Johnson was educated at Camberwell Grammar School and then gained employment as a clerk. During this period, he served four years with the Senior Cadets, attaining the rank of sergeant. He enlisted in July 1915 at the age of eighteen, joining C Company, 31st Battalion, with whom he embarked for Egypt in November 1915. After further training in Egypt, Ralph set sail with the battalion from Alexandria, bound for Marseilles and the battlefields. As with many of the men from the 5th Division, Fromelles was to be his first and only action on the Western Front.

Johnson's individual role in the battle has not been documented and the circumstances of his death are unknown. However, his files reveal a litany of confusion and misinterpretation surrounding the investigation into his burial. He was recorded at the outset as having been killed in action on 21 July 1916, though he was never listed as missing and his remains were never located.

The first oddity was that, according to both the Australian Roll of Honour and Commonwealth War Graves Commission, the official date of his death was the day after the battle, when the fighting had ceased. On a German death list received by the Allies and dated 4 November 1916, Johnson was said to have died on 19 July 1916. It turns out that Johnson was one of a large number of 31st Battalion men who were incorrectly listed as having been killed on 21 July and whose names do not appear on the VC Corner Memorial but somewhere else instead. There has not been an official reason for this oversight, but it's plausible to assume that it was the soonest date after the battle when the battalion was able to check the roll. All those unaccounted for were nominally allotted the 21st.

Further supporting the contention that he was buried at

Pheasant Wood, the Germans sent Johnson's identity disc back to his relatives in 1917 and, at the conclusion of the war, death vouchers were located in the Imperial Prussian War Office also indicating he had fallen in the neighbourhood of Fromelles on 19 July 1916.

What happened next was much harder to explain.

A letter written from Base Records to the Prime Minister's Department in 1922 clearly indicated that there had been discussions dating back to 1920 regarding the final resting place of Ralph Johnson. The letter suggested that Johnson had died as a prisoner of war on 21 July and was buried by the Germans in the Beaucamps Communal Cemetery German Extension. This did not tally with recorded German documentation or with other cases of this nature. We were able to refer to a number of confirmed instances when Australians died as prisoners of war shortly after the battle, and in all the files the specific date and location of their burial in a German cemetery was accurately recorded.

Some months later, we finally uncovered the information regarding Johnson's whereabouts tucked away with several completely unrelated documents in a file titled 'Removal of bodies to Australia – Graves in Germany' at the National Archives of Australia. In correspondence to the Department of Defence dated January 1920, Johnson's father forwarded the translation of a letter he had received from Munich a few months previously, written by a former German soldier, Johann Fischer:

Dear Mr Johnson,
By instructions of the late Ralph Johnson I want to fulfill his

last will and my Christian duty to give you, dear Mr Johnson,
the sad news that he succumbed on 19 July 1916 at eight in the
evening, near Fromelles.

He died for his country and honour to his memory. He lies
in a Bavarian soldiers cemetery in Beaucamps, where he was
buried at my request. I found him still breathing, bandaged
his wounds and during this he asked that I should send you
news. He handed me the letters he carried with him and while
doing so passed away peacefully into the Lord's quiet. Dear Sir,
I would have let you reach certainty before and have tried so
three times, but always my letters came back, because the fron-
tiers were closed and nothing without control was allowed into
neutral countries.

I hardly know whether I am doing right but I want as I
promised him, to give his letters only into his parents hands and
that is why I send you first a passport and letter of him and beg
of you to write to me at once, if possible in German language, if
you are the father. There is also a photo of an elderly gentleman
with it, the rest I keep till I have news.

I beg your forgiveness because of my long silence.

This emotionally charged letter from the man who claimed to
have buried their son would have fuelled the family's hope that his
remains might yet be found. Attempts were made by the Imperial
War Graves Commission to contact Fischer, but it wasn't until
1922 that he was traced to the town of Amberg in Bavaria.

The local town magistrate was requested to obtain a statement from Fischer, but the reply received by the Commission

contained very little detail and hinted that the former Bavarian soldier was disowning his previous account, making lame excuses as to why the grave might not be found after all:

> *The moulder, Johann Fischer, declared on being questioned that he could make no further statement than that Johnson was buried in the Bavarian Military Cemetery in Beaucamps. He does not know the number of the grave. Fischer suggests it is possible that the grave may later have been destroyed by shellfire as the burial took place in 1916. He cannot give further particulars.*

In a final effort to elicit a more accurate location from Fischer, a representative of the Commission was sent to Amberg to interview him. At the meeting, the representative produced a plan of the cemetery at Beaucamps, and Fischer marked the spot where he said he'd interred Johnson's body. However, a search of the cemetery turned up no trace of its existence, and when the plot itself was excavated, there were no remains of Johnson or anyone else. A memorandum to the Prime Minister's Department dated 1924 confirmed that:

> *I have now to inform you that a further communication has been received from the Imperial War Graves Commission stating that all British bodies have now been exhumed from Beaucamps Communal Cemetery German Extension and reburied at Pont du Hem Military Cemetery, La Gorgue and that during the work of exhumation nothing was found which could be connected to the burial of Pte. Johnson.*

As a result, it was decided that a 'special memorial' headstone be erected at Pont du Hem Military Cemetery explaining the suspected circumstances of his burial. His parents were sent the text of this memorial: 'To the memory of this Australian soldier who died as a Prisoner of War and is believed to have been buried at the time in Beaucamps Communal Cemetery German Extension, but whose grave is now lost. Their glory shall not be blotted out.'

Intriguingly, although still recorded as a special memorial, Johnson's headstone no longer bears this inscription – if indeed it ever did.

There is an alternative explanation to this mystifying case. We had already established that the official German documentation regarding Johnson was identical to that of all the other men buried at Pheasant Wood and that it was unusual for the Germans to not accurately record the burial location of a prisoner of war. Our focus shifted to the credibility of Fischer's statements.

One glaring inconsistency continued to plague us. Fischer clearly stated that Johnson died on the battlefield at 8 p.m. on 19 July. It was highly unlikely that a soldier manning the front trenches would be given permission to take the body of an enemy soldier kilometres behind the lines for a proper burial, and well nigh inconceivable that he would deliberately absent himself for this same purpose in the midst of a raging battle.

There is little doubt that Fischer came in contact with Johnson, because at some point he took possession of Johnson's belongings. It is also feasible that the Bavarian soldier found

Johnson on the battlefield – perhaps he may even have been the one to inflict the mortal wound. Whether to fulfil a dying man's promise or simply as a response to post-war guilt, Fischer felt compelled to write to Johnson's father after the war. But the guarded contents of his letter and undeniable reluctance to provide important details suggest that his account of providing an enemy soldier with an honourable grave was possibly just an attempt to offer comfort to Johnson's family and alleviate the pain of their loss. He did not realise that this well-intentioned lie might come back to haunt him. Later, under mounting pressure, Fischer may have felt obliged to add to it further by pinpointing an imaginary location.

It was therefore our contention, supported by German documentation of the time, that 715 Lance Corporal Ralph Johnson did not die as a prisoner of war on 21 July 1916 and was never buried at Beaucamps Communal Cemetery German Extension. All available evidence pointed to the fact that he was likely to have been one of the 250 Australian and British soldiers buried in the mass graves at Pheasant Wood, but we have yet to locate a descendant so that his identity can be confirmed.

3006 CORPORAL PERCY GEORGE ARCHIBALD BARR, 54TH BATTALION

Percy Barr was born in Oxford, England, but in 1903, at the age of six, he moved to Australia with his parents, where they settled in Dulwich Hill, Sydney. He was educated at Arnold College,

Petersham, and after serving four years in the Senior Cadets and another one with the Citizen Military Forces, Barr enlisted with the 10th Reinforcements, 2nd Battalion, in July 1915. Upon arrival in Egypt in February 1916, he was re-assigned to the 54th Battalion during the reshuffle of troops after the Gallipoli campaign. Some weeks before he left for France in June 1916, Percy was promoted to the rank of corporal.

Less than a month after his arrival on the Western Front, Percy Barr participated in the battle at Fromelles. In statements later taken by the Red Cross, some members of his battalion stated that he had been killed by shellfire in the German lines and that his body had to be abandoned when the Australians were forced to retreat.

A search of his files revealed that his name was one of those recorded on the German death list dated 4 November 1916 and that his identity disc was located after the war in German possession. Furthermore, German death vouchers were also found indicating that Barr had fallen at Fromelles on 19 July 1916.

Everything pointed to the possibility that Barr was one of those buried at Pheasant Wood, except for the inexplicable fact that in 1920 he was listed on a Graves Registration concentration report as being interred at Rue du Bois Military Cemetery. We tried to locate cemetery records at the Commonwealth War Graves Commission, but apparently many of the burial returns were scrapped during the Second World War, presumably as part of the recycling drive to aid the war effort. With no means to determine the circumstances surrounding his apparent recovery, there was no way we could assess the veracity of its likelihood.

We did establish that Barr's grave has only ever been inscribed as 'Believed to be' and was never formally confirmed to contain his actual remains. Strangely, his mother was offered the same option to have those words omitted from his headstone and, like Scott's mother, she agreed, but for some unknown reason they were never removed. Further complications arose when it was ascertained that two other soldiers named Barr were killed in no-man's-land at Fromelles and neither body was ever recovered. This means that the body at Rue du Bois could equally have been that of 3011A Private George Hamilton Barr or 3474A Private David Barr.

1137 CORPORAL WALTER GODFREY HUGHES, 54TH BATTALION

Born in South Melbourne, Victoria, Walter Hughes was a 43-year-old station overseer–accountant living with his wife in Moore Park, Sydney, when he enlisted very early in the war with the 1st Reinforcements, 2nd Battalion. Shortly after the battalion arrived in Egypt, Walter Hughes took part in the landing at Anzac Cove in April 1915. He went on to serve throughout the entire Gallipoli campaign.

Like Percy Barr, Hughes was re-assigned to the 54th Battalion after the withdrawal from Gallipoli and travelled to France in June 1916, taking part in the Battle of Fromelles less than a month later. Listed as missing after the battle, he was not confirmed as killed in action until his identity disc was returned by the Germans in 1917, even though his name had appeared on the German death list dated 4 November 1916.

The only report of his death comes from a member of the 54th Battalion who said he had seen Hughes killed by rifle fire just beyond the Australian trench. This story was never verified by corroborating statements and therefore cannot be considered entirely reliable. German death vouchers located after the war at the Imperial Prussian War Office confirmed that Hughes had been killed in the neighbourhood of Fromelles on 19 July 1916, strongly indicating the enemy had taken possession of his body after the battle.

Again, enquiries with the Commonwealth War Graves Commission revealed that the burial returns for Ration Farm Military Cemetery (about 1.5 kilometres north of Pheasant Wood) have been destroyed, and we are none the wiser with regards to the supposed discovery of his remains. All we have is a Graves Registration concentration report in Hughes' service file detailing his apparent burial at Ration Farm in 1920 and a note regarding a photograph taken of the headstone after his reburial.

Without the burial returns, it is hard to determine whether the Germans might have given Hughes a separate battlefield grave that was later discovered and exhumed by the Graves Registration Unit. Nevertheless, in the absence of evidence that either proves or disproves the circumstances of his burial, we must consider the established criteria for inclusion on the Department of Defence's working list of names. Clearly, he falls into the first three of those categories and so should be added as possibly being one of those buried in the mass graves at Pheasant Wood.

1916 PRIVATE ARTHUR FRANCIS ENGEL, 60TH BATTALION

Arthur Engel was born in 1893 at Echuca, Victoria, to New Zealand emigrants Arthur and Catherine Engel. He lived with his parents in Prahran, Melbourne, and was employed as a labourer until his enlistment in June 1915. He joined the 3rd Reinforcements, 23rd Battalion, in October 1915 and saw out the final months of the Gallipoli campaign with them until he was admitted to hospital in December with trench foot, frostbite and influenza. Back in Egypt, Engel joined the 60th Battalion and was sent to France in June 1916.

In the pandemonium of battle, no record of his final moments exist, and immediately afterwards he was posted as missing in action. It was not until 13 September 1916 that his name appeared on a German death list and notification released that his personal effects were in German hands (his identity disc was returned to his family in 1921). At first, it was mis-interpreted that he had died as a prisoner of war in Germany, but this was later elucidated to mean that he had been killed in action at Fromelles on 19 July 1916. The German death vouchers and associated documents located after the war and reproduced in both his service file and Red Cross records verify these details.

The first mention of a burial for Arthur Engel was in 1920, when the Graves Registration Unit noted it in his file. His family was informed, and the offer of a headstone photograph substantiated that authorities thought him to be buried at Ration Farm. Unfortunately, as we have already seen, the burial returns for Ration Farm no longer exist, and there is no way we can establish how his recovery and identification were made.

Like Hughes, it was possible that Engel's remains may have been recovered from an unmarked individual grave set apart from those at Pheasant Wood, but without further evidence to prove this, and with the records meeting the necessary criteria for inclusion, he also had to be considered as potentially one of the men buried in the mass graves.

Chapter 13
HONOURED REST

Soldiers, hear our cry.
We cry in grief for your loss so long ago, and in joy on your return today.

From address by Her Excellency Ms Quentin Bryce AC, Governor General of Australia, on the occasion of dedication at Fromelles (Pheasant Wood) Military Cemetery, 19 July 2010

Like many young men in 1915, Fred Dyson originally wanted to join the smart, dapper and highly fashionable Australian Light Horse. Excited by the thought of going to war with a plume in his hat and a fine steed to bear him into battle, he must have been bitterly disappointed when he failed the horsemanship riding test. Thoughts of mounted parades and glorious cavalry charges were soon replaced by the harsh reality that war for an infantryman was little more than mechanised slaughter on an industrial scale.

Fromelles was a long way away from the nineteen-year-old's home at Sherwood, New South Wales. Situated on the Macleay River in the mid-north-coast region of the state, the timber cottage on the family's property in Lovelocks Creek Road had been Fred's base all his life, until late 1915, when he signed up for the infantry.

With his comrades of the 54th Battalion, Fred set out across the fields on that fateful July night, and managed to negotiate no-man's-land and reach the German front lines. Grimly holding his ground, he turned to dress the injuries of his wounded mate, Private David Chapman, before resuming his place in the line. Moments later, he was dead:

> *On 19th July at Fleurbaix I* [Chapman] *was hit while taking part in a charge. Dyson was alongside and bound up my wounds. A few minutes later Dyson was struck by a shell and died instantly. He was right alongside me at the time. This was about half past six in the evening.*

I was fortunate enough to watch the first burial as it took place on a frosty January morning in 2010 and afterwards wrote down my impressions.

It was an extraordinarily beautiful scene, with the snow-covered cemetery stretched out silent beneath the blue Fromelles sky. To the side, beyond the boundary wall, a small but resolute group of mourners braved the gnawing chill, staunchly committed to paying their last respects. Soldiers from the Australian and British Armies, rugged up in uniform coats and gloves, slid the polished timber coffin from the hearse and shouldered it with care. At a slow march, they solemnly conveyed their precious cargo through the archway and into the cemetery grounds.

The chaplains waited patiently at the foot of a single open grave situated at the front of the cemetery. The dark gaping hole was a stark contrast to the clean white carpet of snow surrounding it. With precise military efficiency and an unmistakable air of reverence, the soldiers placed the coffin across the grave and stood back beneath the Cross of Sacrifice.

Once the simple prayers were said, the coffin was gently lowered into the ground to the strains of the last post. In an apt farewell, the restored vintage cornet that sounded the final piece had once accompanied the men of the doomed 5th Division. I found out later that the current owner, Peter Nelson, saw it on eBay for sale, recognised its significance and gladly purchased it for a reasonable price. Approaching its centenary and looking every one of its years, the battered cornet of the 31st Battalion performed with all the gravity and soul befitting the occasion.

To finish, a crisp volley of rifle fire echoed across the frozen fields, heralding the end of the momentous ceremony. All but forgotten in a French field since 1916, the first soldier of Pheasant Wood had now been buried with full military honours in the new Fromelles (Pheasant Wood) Military Cemetery.

At the time, no one was aware who this first soldier actually was. We now know from DNA testing that, after nearly ninety-four years, Fred Dyson had finally been laid to rest in the honourable grave that he had always deserved.

Throughout February 2010, a further 248 sets of remains were buried in the cemetery built specifically for them. Only one did not yet meet his final resting place. It was decided that one set of remains be kept back so that the final burial would occur during the cemetery dedication service on the anniversary of the battle.

Every morning, there was an opening ceremony where flags were raised and lowered to half-mast. Then followed the daily burials, with an individual service for every soldier. The day concluded with a rifle volley and a sombre rendition of the last post.

With all the men now recovered and reburied, focus shifted to the forthcoming announcement of the identities. By now, everyone knew that the extraction of DNA had been overwhelmingly successful, as nearly every set of remains had yielded viable samples. The research of the Fromelles Descendant Database assisted in locating a large number of descendants who then registered with the Department of Defence. Sandra and I were eager to know if our four and a half years of hard work had been justified.

The first sitting of the Joint Identification Board began in March 2010. Composed of government appointees from both the Australian and British military, in addition to relevant subject-matter experts, it was the board's task to assess all the gathered forensic evidence for each set of remains and determine whether it was enough to make a positive identification. Slowly and methodically, they analysed the DNA results and compared them with the corresponding anthropological and archaeological finds.

The day before the official announcement, unconfirmed reports began to circulate. Staff of the Australian Fromelles

Project Group were telephoning descendants to inform them that their soldier had been positively identified. Joyous emails and voice messages of delight and gratitude poured in. Sandra and I could rest easy, for the results were showing us that every second of our labours had been worth it.

A few years ago, I took leave from my position in the Victorian Police to enable my partner to take up a fantastic career opportunity in Queensland. Although my job's emphasis on administration had always been a drawback, there have been times when I have missed the particular stimulation that came with it. Nevertheless, I couldn't help comparing the phone calls I would have to make as a police officer – informing someone that a person close to them had been arrested or hurt or even killed – with the calls I made to the newly identified Fromelles descendants. It's almost impossible to describe some of the ecstatic responses to the news that a relative had been matched with their DNA. It was like they had won the lottery! In terms of 'job satisfaction', nothing else has come close.

Although there was more than ten years between them, the three Wilson brothers – Samuel, Eric (known as 'Booma' to his family) and Jim – were inseparable at home and at war. Together, they worked alongside their father at a timber mill in Port Macquarie, and together they arrived in France with VII Platoon, B Company, of the 53rd Battalion.

Three weeks later, at Fromelles, two were dead, the other was severely wounded and a family back home was grief-stricken.

Jim was the first to fall, shot through the neck in no-man's-land during the initial assault. Although he was rescued from the field and eventually taken to hospital in England, where he recuperated from his wound, for many weeks his family did not know that he had survived. The two elder brothers made it as far as the enemy lines but we only have eyewitness descriptions of what happened to Sam. In the early hours of the morning, the Germans were making repeated counter-attacks, and reluctantly the Australians had to give ground. Defending his position as a lone rear guard, Sam was last seen by Private Eli Taylor holding off the enemy while his mates escaped:

> He was bombing Germans in a trench when about fifty of them rushed out at him. He waited until they got quite near and then threw his remaining bombs down between himself and them.
>
> He held at bay a German party attempting to come down a sap while a number of other men were able to get away. He held the sap all alone and was himself killed by a bomb when the others had safely got away.

Considering how devoted the three brothers were to each other, it is not too difficult to imagine that Eric may already have been killed or wounded and that Sam stayed behind, refusing to abandon him. This possibility became ever more plausible when news of the identifications was announced.

Whether by coincidence or a conscious act of compassion by their enemies, the two brothers were recovered, incredibly, lying side by side in the mass graves. Those involved in the exhumation were oblivious to their identities but still re-interred the bodies side by side in the new cemetery.

In mid-March, the Joint Identification Board released the first list of soldiers who had been positively named, and the remarkable story of the Wilson brothers came to light. For their descendants, it was final closure on a dreadful family tragedy. Esther Gray, niece of the Wilson brothers, was overwhelmed: 'I got the call from the Australian Army early in the morning, and when they told me I stood there and I could not believe it . . . it was just so emotional. Their family suffered so much grief in not knowing. They passed on the need to know where they were.'

The Wilson family had never given up hope of finding the two brothers. At last, after almost a century, they could lay the remains of their ancestors to rest and with them dispel the crippling grief that had consumed the boys' mother, Isabella, when she learned of their deaths. She died soon after of a broken heart.

In addition to the Wilson brothers, seventy-five men were restored their names, and in the coming months more followed.

Bob Green's descendants were elated. Our search for them had been one of the most rewarding for us. Teresa Westerling, Bob's great-niece, told us:

We had a phone call from Canberra this morning. We are truly excited and the phone has been red hot with conversations to the 'new' wing of the family. The rest of her family are delighted. We have also let the Humann family know. To be able to go over

there and know he existed and to see a grave marked with his
name will be a very humbling experience.

Not only had different branches of the family been reunited but they had also taken it upon themselves to go even further and locate the family of Bob's best friend. In this way, they discovered what became of Bob's beloved fiancée, Nancie Pearson. After mourning Bob's loss, she eventually moved away from Western Australia to the bustling metropolis of Sydney. There, she met and eventually married local fishmonger Reginald Taylor. The couple went on to have two sons, the second of whom they named Robert.

Also identified was the brawling rugby utility back Herbert 'Nutsy' Bolt, who had taken on an unbeatable number of Germans with bayonet and fist. His family were overjoyed to have found him, as Robert Bolt, Nutsy's eldest living descendant, explained: 'I am absolutely ecstatic. The whole family is thrilled that he will now have his own marked grave, because that is what he, and all of them, deserve.'

It was particularly satisfying for us that Robert Scott was among the identified. Verifying our suspicions about his incorrectly named grave at Rue-Petillon Military Cemetery, it strengthened the probability that others such as Ralph Johnson, Percy Barr, Walter Hughes and Arthur Engel had been mistakenly identified and buried after the war. Scott was one of only a few men who were identified without the benefit of DNA sampling. In his case, a battered home-made metal identity disc was found with his body, the age range and dimensions of which

matched his enlistment file. His DNA file was also consist-
ent with a type common in Scotland at the turn of the century.
Scott's family were only located after he was identified, and
Jeanette Inglis, whose grandmother was Robert Scott's aunt, told
us of past grief: 'I remember my grandmother often talking about
poor Bertie who went away down the farm road and never came
home. We feel a line has been drawn under unfinished history.'

Reverend Holliday, Theo Pflaum and Sir James Burns spent
many futile years trying to locate the whereabouts of their sons.
Now, generations later and long after they too had passed away,
their quest was fulfilled. All three of the boys had been found.

And there were more. Looking down the list of names, I
realised how many of their stories I knew and how each had
taken on characteristics and personalities of their own. They
had become like family, and it felt more important than ever
to share what we had learned about their lives with others. The
adopted Leslie Leister, who had proved such an enigma, was on
the list, and so too were Vic Momplhait and Allan Bennett, who
had been hit when he went out to rescue Bob Green. Maurice
Corigliano, who had sensed disaster and farewelled his family
with a foreboding postcard before the battle, was also named.

For Tim Whitford, the identification of Harry Willis was the
fulfilment of a promise he had made to himself and his family.
Having stood by Lambis from almost the beginning of his journey, he was taken completely unawares by the wave of emotion
that swept over him: 'You have all these defence mechanisms
in your heart . . . in my heart and in my head I believed it but
when I got the call, I just couldn't stop shaking.'

The following month, a further list of nineteen names was released, and then in July another two. More lives were being restored, and among them were Robert Dewar, Ignatius Norris and Aime Verpillot, the Swiss immigrant who had rushed through his Australian citizenship just so he could enlist.

In April 2011 the Joint Identification Board named another fourteen men, and in May 2012 nine more were added to the list of 119. In an odd twist to the tale, one of the graves previously thought to contain the remains of one of the three unknown British soldiers was found to actually hold the remains of 3256 Private Maurice Reid of the 32nd Battalion. This leaves only two possible unknown British soldiers from the total of 250. Perhaps they too might turn out to be Australian. Only time will tell.

In total contrast to the first burial at Fromelles in January 2010, the final one took place on a stiflingly hot day in July of that year. Flanked by temporary stands filled with descendants and guests furiously fanning themselves with printed Orders of Service, the new cemetery was awash with colour and life. International dignitaries took their places on the plinth below the Cross of Sacrifice and awaited the arrival of the coffin.

Shimmering in the heat, four horses with gleaming ebony coats waited beside the cool green canopy of Pheasant Wood, patiently hitched to the gun carriage bearing the last set of remains. From here – the original resting place of all the men – they slowly made the short journey to the cemetery, where the last unknown soldier was laid to rest. With much pomp, ceremony and heartfelt speeches, the cemetery was dedicated.

Up in the stands amid the crowds of kin, Bob Green's descendants turned to the family seated next to them and enquired which soldier they were there to represent. They were astounded to learn that they were the relatives of Allan Bennett – the very same soldier who risked and ultimately gave his life carrying a mortally wounded Green to safety. But in my mind, this was no coincidence. There are unseen hands purposefully guiding these many quirks of fate. The world had finally turned and the circle is complete.

Now those who were missing can lie forever in the sympathetic embrace of a small French village, the name of which has become synonymous with their passing. The words of the mayor of Fromelles, Hubert Huchette, confirm that our soldiers are in good hands: 'By welcoming these soldiers to the heart of our village we wish to weave threads of friendship with their families, their friends; we wish to remember daily what they have done for our country.'

Curiously blank, but with the same sense of dignity as the recently identified graves, stand 131 white headstones. Each represents an individual story woven into the fabric of a grieving family, every one a paragraph from our past, and together a chapter of sacrifice in Australian history. In the years ahead, through continued advocacy and patient research, perhaps one day they too will have their names restored and their lives recognised.

Chapter 14

ENDINGS AND
BEGINNINGS

Death is not extinguishing the light; it is putting out the lamp because
the dawn has come.

Rabindranath Tagore, philosopher and Nobel laureate

Every year, as 19 July approaches, news stories appear about the
anniversary of the battle at Fromelles. No doubt the centenary
of the battle in 2016 will attract a fresh storm of media attention, as it should do. Much is made of the recent discovery, for
Lambis's search is an astonishing tale in itself, but it highlights
the inescapable fact that, up until recently, this was an event
that had been relegated to the footnotes of Australian history.

Some would argue that it only deserves minor status in
the general scheme of the war because, effectively, neither side
gained ground, nor did it have any real bearing on the course of
the conflict. And yet, there were more Australian casualties sustained in twenty-four hours at Fromelles than in the whole of

Brunswick Street,
New Farm,
Brisbane,
AUSTRALIA.

To Officer in Charge,
    Base Records,
        A.I.F. Headquarters Horseferry Road,
            LONDON.

Dear Sir,

           I am writing to inquire of my son John Joseph
GOULDING, No. 555. B. Company. 31st Battalion, A.I.F. who
was reported missing since July 19th 1916.   I have not received
anything belonging to him but disc was sent from Germany sometime
during 1917 with a promise that further inquiries would be
made and I would be notified.   Have heard no further of him.
I have waited patiently with a aching heart for news of him
if only I could know that he did not suffer too much from the
Huns if he fell in their hands which I have reasons to believe
during that dreadful slaughter of Fleur-Bay of which thousands
of Australian Mothers has reasons to think seriously.   My son
left Australia to do his bit for the country he was born in
England.   He did not stand long but I do hope that something
further will be made known to me although three years has
passed it seems but as yesterday. Iam still waiting.
           First missing, then Prisoner of war then killed in
action.   I know he was not the only one by thousands but he was
my son just lent to me for 35 years and then missing.   I know
a good son, I believe a good man but do not know if a good
soldier.   He has paid the price as many others have done but
in all the world their is no love like a mothers love for her
children if she is ever so poor, if a true woman.
           I have been trying to be patient for three years
hoping but just today I thought perhaps you have forgotten
but this I know that the war has just begun for mothers that
dearly loved their boys all over the world.   God help them
to bear it.   The suspence is what makes it so hard.   Hoping
this mail will bring some tidings or the next but one.
           I cannot write more and I know you don't want to
read more.   May I please ask will you try and find out if any
record of him, my boy, and oblige

           (Sgd) Mrs. J. Alice Goulding.

the Boer War, Korean War and Vietnam War combined. The official line that the Battle of Fromelles was merely a part of the larger Battle of the Somme is no longer acceptable. The day is coming when Fromelles will be widely recognised alongside all the other great defeats and victories that tell the story of our nation.

With the gift of hindsight, we can now discern the immediate impact that the battle had on countless numbers of people. The men who were killed in the fighting and the tremendous potential that was lost along with them. The survivors who were shattered by the ordeal and never truly recovered. The families back home who had to deal with a returned soldier with severe physical and/or deep psychological wounds. And the families who lost their loved one and never found out what became of him.

Even as I write this, an absolutely heartbreaking letter has come to my attention for the first time. Sent to the authorities in 1919 by the mother of one of the soldiers recently identified through DNA testing (Private John Joseph Goulding), the letter encapsulates, in the simplest of terms, the plight of so many women in her position: 'I have been trying to be patient for three years hoping but just today I thought perhaps you have forgotten . . . this I know; that the war has just begun for mothers who dearly loved their boys all over the world. God help them to bear it.'

It's important not to forget the people of Fromelles, who returned to their village at the end of the war to find it was all but obliterated. After four years of German occupation, the buildings were rubble, the streets were choked with barbed wire and abandoned fortifications, and the fields were strewn with unexploded shells and the bones of the dead. It took many years for the locals to return to some sort of normality, and, today, commemorating the battle and honouring the Allies – especially the Australians – who fell there is a visible part of community life. In addition to the excellent Fromelles Museum set up in the Town Hall, the prominent Commonwealth cemeteries close by, the monuments (including the famous Cobbers statue) and the scattering of Australian-themed shops and cafes, the local primary school has been renamed 'L'École des Cobbers' and is adorned with a kangaroo weathervane. Plans for an interpretive centre are also nearing completion.

Then there are the victors. Although their casualty list was in the vicinity of 1500 men, the decisive victory must have been a tremendous boost to German morale. Many of the 500 Allied soldiers who were captured were paraded through the streets of Lille to demonstrate the might of the German Army.

There are wider implications too, when we consider the 27-year-old soldier who witnessed his countrymen repel a determined force that had travelled halfway across the world to defeat them. The conquest no doubt made an impression on Lance Corporal Adolf Hitler of the 16th Bavarian Reserve Infantry Regiment, stationed at Fromelles in July 1916. Hitler was a despatch runner, whose hazardous task was to carry messages from the front line to headquarters, and it's intriguing to note that, during the battle, his regiment was situated opposite the Australians.

Clearly, it stayed with the future dictator because, as soon as France surrendered to Germany in June 1940, Hitler went immediately to Fromelles and toured the battlefield, taking in the cement blockhouse where he sheltered during the Australians' attack. In 1942, he arranged for a special plaque to be attached to the wall of the billet near Fournes commemorating the fact that he had stayed there a quarter of a century before. (Although it was badly damaged after the war, the Adolf Hitler plaque has now been restored and is on display for all to see at the Fromelles Museum.)

The man who would lead the world into a second catastrophic conflict just over two decades later was unquestionably affected by what happened at Fromelles, though just how much his experience influenced what came after we will probably never know.

From time to time, discussions arise in the contemporary media surrounding the issue of recovering human remains when the life itself has long been extinguished. Stories about grieving relatives who 'cannot rest' and 'lack closure' until their loved one has been properly buried can arouse heated debate, depending on the individual moral standpoint. Reopening 'cold cases' has become a popular subject of bestselling books, films and television series, with the creators exploiting the limitless dramatic potential when people (usually involved in law enforcement) seek to relieve the suffering of those left behind.

As a police officer, I have witnessed the far-reaching effects when the body of a victim of accident or foul play has not been recovered. When family members are deprived of knowing the whereabouts of the final resting place, the suffering is immense. It's as if the terrible circumstances of the victim's death are intensified when their earthly remains have not been interred in a location of safety and peace where the bereaved can pay their respects and express their love and loss.

The accounts of the grieving families and friends of the lost soldiers of Fromelles as they described the agonies of 'not knowing' seemed just as raw and devastating as if they had happened yesterday, even though those people are now themselves passed away. Strangely, I have sometimes found myself experiencing a greater empathy for the ancestors of our past than I do for the victims of today. In my job, I learned to distance myself from the horror and anguish I witnessed, as a coping mechanism more than anything else. But I have found myself deeply affected by the bereaved families of Fromelles.

Perhaps it has to do with the overwhelming impact the war had on Australia – pre-war innocence being replaced with post-war trauma – and the fact that my own flesh and blood played a small part in its shaping. Or maybe it has to do with the unbridled enthusiasm of so many Australians who volunteered – whether by love of country, awareness of duty or a youthful sense of adventure – for a conflict the scale of which they could never have imagined nor prepared for. And yet, despite all the harsh realities of modern warfare, they remained resolute and continued to willingly offer their own personal sacrifice. Ultimately, I suspect it's a combination of the two.

Diary notes, Tim Lycett, January 2010
It's so still and silent, you can hear the snow crunching under the soldiers' feet as they pace solemnly in time across the frozen ground. The weight on their shoulders is not a burden for they carry one of their own and bear him with pride. One by one, a steady stream of draped coffins are carried into the peaceful confines of the cemetery and laid to their final rest with the honour they deserve.

I know their names. And now by delving into their history, I have inevitably come to know about their lives and the lives of their families. I just never anticipated the emotional bond I would feel with this generation of men so far removed from my own.

The recitation of Binyon's 'For the Fallen' cannot fail to touch the hearts of the assembled crowd:

They shall grow not old, as we that are left grow old:
Age shall not weary them, nor the years condemn.
At the going down of the sun and in the morning,
We will remember them.
And as one we respond: 'Lest we forget.'

I close my eyes and see the sepia-tinted faces in the photographs that are as familiar as old friends. These men were lawyers, teachers, policemen, farmers, labourers, shearers, clerks, and, yes, some of them were still children. Soldiering was a sudden interruption to their ordinary lives, thrust upon them by circumstance and world events beyond their control.

The sharp report of a rifle volley pierces the clean crisp air . . .

I imagine that I can hear their voices drifting on the wind,

calling out across the recesses of time. For me, recovering and
identifying their remains is still only half the job done. Giving
them a name on a headstone is just not enough. To truly do
their memories justice, I believe we need to find out something
of their lives, not just the circumstances of their deaths.
    The last strains of the bugle echo across the still fields . . .
    I think of all the loss. Not only have these men been lost to
us in a physical sense, so their stories are also vanishing.
    A new sense of purpose blooms within me.

Watching the first burial at the new cemetery was more than
just a deeply affecting occasion for me. It also stands out clearly
in my mind as the moment when I decided to share what I have
learned about the men of Pheasant Wood and my experience of
coming to know them. Having read so many books about the
Great War, I made a decision that it was now time to write one
of my own.

At the beginning of this narrative, I spoke about my grandfather
whose experience in the Great War first inspired my interest.
Through the years that I worked on the Fromelles project, he
was never far from my thoughts. I would find myself linking the
experiences of the men that I was researching to the descriptions
in my grandfather's diary. Sometimes, it would occur to me that
a soldier I was tracing had been at the exact place at the exact
time that Pa had been there, and I would feel certain that they
must have met. This made it all very real and personal for me.

My grandfather was a man of strict principles who was devoted to his family. Rarely one to display emotions, in his final years he occasionally let his guard down and showed his youngest grandson a softer and more caring side to his character. I have no doubt he would have given his wholehearted blessing to my involvement in this project.

Back in the days when I first began to do committed research, one of my priorities was finding out what happened to Pa's brother, Fred, whose faded portrait he kept on display until the day he died. In July 1917, nineteen-year-old Fred reached Belgium on the Western Front and joined the 46th Battalion in reserve among the underground catacombs of Hill 63 near Ploegsteert Wood. Eight days later, they were only hours away from being withdrawn from the lines. During the night, there was some enemy shelling on Hill 63 and Fred was killed. The battalion diary records the event: 'On the night of 17th/18th Hill 63 was heavily shelled for 4½ hours by gas shells, shrapnel and high explosive. Very few casualties.'

I was seized with indignation when I read those words. One of those 'very few casualties' was my great-uncle. Surely his death deserved more than two brief lines? I suppose the person who made the entry had become accustomed to the parade of victims and would have no sense that, decades later, a descendant of one of the dead might be upset by his glib summary of the event. It reminded me of the spirit of Remarque's classic novel, *All Quiet on the Western Front*, about the relentless brutality of life and death in the Great War. These days, it also brings me back to the official army communiqué mentioned at the end

of Chapter 3, which dismisses the bloodbath of the Battle of
Fromelles as 'important raids' in which Australians 'took part'.

There's one more story that I love to tell, which demonstrates the 'ripple effect' of how one person's experience at
Fromelles went on – albeit in a roundabout way – to inspire an
iconic contemporary Australian image. In Chapter 3, there is a
graphic description of the battlefield from one of the soldiers of
the 53rd Battalion, John Gotch Ridley (whose father was a partner in the oldest publications distributing company in Australia,
Gordon and Gotch). John Ridley survived the wounds he sustained at Fromelles and returned to service, where he was later
awarded promotion and military honours.

After the war, he returned to Australia and entered the
Baptist ministry. Then his wartime experiences caught up with
him and he suffered a nervous breakdown. Upon his recovery, he decided to become an outback missionary. Although
he would always suffer from the effects of his wounds, his
health gradually returned and he embraced the life of a travelling evangelist, gaining quite a reputation throughout Australia,
preaching at conventions and churches.

And this is where his story becomes especially intriguing. In
November 1932, he was preaching at a Baptist church in Sydney
about the 'Echoes of Eternity', based on Isaiah 57:15. A powerful
and charismatic speaker, he was in full flight when he suddenly
fell silent. Laying aside his prepared notes, he raised his eyes to
the heavens and cried, 'Eternity, Eternity! I wish that I could
sound or shout that word to everyone in the streets of Sydney!'

Seated in the audience that night was an illiterate petty

criminal named Arthur Stace. The former alcoholic had recently converted to Christianity, and so moved was he by Ridley's words that, after the sermon had finished, he walked outside, produced a piece of chalk he happened to have in his pocket and, even though he could barely form the letters of his own name, wrote the word 'Eternity' in perfect copperplate on the pavement.

Stace (now more commonly known as 'Mr Eternity') continued to echo Ridley's message for the remaining thirty-five years of his life and has been attributed with writing 'Eternity' on Sydney streets more than 500 000 times. In an ultimate tribute to his work, the Sydney Harbour Bridge was lit up with fireworks forming Stace's distinctive word to celebrate the turn of the century in 2000. The image was seen by millions of people around the world.

There are those who might argue that Ridley's collective war experience was responsible for his evangelical fervour, not just one single battle. But any doubt about the profound effect that 19 July 1916 had on him must be called into question by the fact that when this wandering preacher finally settled down in Pennant Hills, Sydney, he named his new home 'Fromelles'.

Though Sandra and I both had a strong sense of 'remembrance' prior to embarking on the Fromelles project, there's no doubt that this work has made us look far more deeply into the impact of the war at a community level. It has defined the importance of knowing where we come from as a way of helping us to understand where we are now and where we might be going.

Research on the descendants continues, albeit at a far more relaxed pace. We do not know how many (or indeed if any) further identifications will be possible, and time is running out, as government funding for the DNA process finishes in 2014. There are a number of cases where we must accept that all avenues for DNA matching have been exhausted, but there is always a slim chance that an unknown descendant will come forward.

I will continue to search for those soldiers whose stories have frustratingly eluded us – though more for personal satisfaction than anything else. Sandra has moved on to other projects but can always be relied upon to assist if new information comes to light.

We are immensely proud of the small part we played in this extraordinary story.

THO' GREAT SEAS DIVIDE US

I saw Jentsch on July 19th at dusk with his head blown off.

3571A Corporal Lawrence Perry, 53rd Battalion

Our Ernie's tour of duty lasted only eight months. He didn't get any military decorations or awards – in fact, he was a pretty unremarkable soldier. Just one of many minor players in the vast battle theatres of the Great War.

Private Ernest Augustus Jentsch was the grandson of a German immigrant. When he sailed from Sydney on the troop ship HMAT *Euripides* on 2 November 1915, he left behind his parents, Alice and Felix, and his sixteen-year-old sister, Muriel. Over the next six months of training in Egypt, he was first promoted to corporal and then to lance sergeant. So he must have done okay!

In June 1916 orders arrived for the 53rd Battalion to proceed to the Western Front. For some bizarre reason, their

commanding officer decided it would be an excellent training exercise for the men to march across the Egyptian desert to
the port of Alexandria in the stifling heat of day. With the soldiers instructed to wear full battle kit, it was a debilitating and
humiliating experience, and many soldiers literally collapsed on
the side of the road. Other battalions more sensibly marched in
the cool of the evening, but on the way they had to pick up the
soldiers of the 53rd who had fallen through sheer exhaustion
during the day.

Ernest eventually boarded ship in Alexandria and arrived in
Marseilles, France, on 28 June 1916. Twenty-one days later, he
was dead, just a month before his twenty-third birthday. This
was not an uncommon thing to happen in the Great War. It's
what happened more than ninety years on that makes his story
so extraordinary. Ernest Jentsch was a '19th of July' soldier. He
was killed at the Battle of Fromelles in 1916, and his body was
buried by the Germans in the mass graves at Pheasant Wood.
Ninety-three years later, the burials were discovered by Lambis
Englezos and his dedicated team.

I first came across Ernest in 2005 on a casualty list. I was
doing some family research into my paternal great-grand-
father, Stanley Bendall, who was also in the 53rd Battalion. The
name 'Jentsch' jumped out at me because it's my maternal great-
grandmother's maiden name. Jentsch is an unusual name, so
it was pretty easy to work out that he was indeed a relative. I
printed out his war record, had a quick read and filed it away
with the rest of our family soldiers.

We didn't know anything about the Battle of Fromelles

back then. The story passed down through my family was that Ernest had been killed in action, and the record showed that his memorial was at VC Corner, Fromelles. I simply accepted the fact that he didn't have a known grave because his remains had never been identified. Like everyone else, I presumed he was buried over there 'somewhere'.

Even so, I promised myself that if I ever travelled to France, I would visit his memorial and lay flowers on behalf of his poor grieving mother. As a mother myself, it was terribly upsetting to read the painfully brief note that Alice sent to Base Records after the war: 'Kindly forward one pamphlet "Graves of the Fallen" to above address.' I guess she just wanted to know where her boy was and prayed he might lie in one of these graves

As if that wasn't enough grief, Alice's nephew Harold Salmon was killed a year later in Belgium and, just as with Ernest, they never found out where he was buried.

The intense sadness I felt for distant kin who lived generations ago took me by surprise. I can only imagine the inconsolable sorrow the family must have experienced at the time. Whenever Anzac Day came around, I would think about the sacrifices made by my forebears, but it wasn't until a couple of years later that Ernest demanded my attention. This was the startling moment when I stumbled across his photo as I was browsing the Australian War Memorial website on Anzac Day in 2009. For the first time, I clapped eyes on the man who was to have such an incredible impact on my life.

The next day, I was thumbing through a newspaper lying on the kitchen bench. There was a tribute article about Australia's heroes who never returned from the war. I was scanning the pages when I was suddenly astounded to see the same handsome portrait of Ernest staring out at me. My first instinct was to find out why he had been featured, so I searched the internet for his name and was amazed to find it among a list of soldiers discovered by Lambis Englezos who were believed to be buried at Pheasant Wood. I had seen Lambis on television and remember thinking how wonderful it would be for the families to locate their long-lost loved ones. It never even remotely occurred to me that a relative of mine might be one of those soldiers. My commitment to finding 'Our Ernest' began at that very moment.

My great-great-grandfather, Paul Gerhard Jentsch, was the older brother of Ernest's father (so he was Ernest's uncle). Paul's daughter, Rosalia Emily, was my great-grandmother (so Ernest's first cousin), and her daughter, Vivienne (Nanna), is my maternal grandmother. In 'simple' terms, Ernest is my first cousin three times removed.

I registered as a relative with the Department of Defence's Fromelles Project Group, believing there would be a host of other Jentsches on their list. To my surprise, at that stage I was the only relative to have lodged my details. I knew DNA was going to be a factor in the identification process, and because my grandmother was the one remaining member of this side of the family still living and only one generation removed, I thought she would be the obvious person to supply the comparative DNA sample. But the project's researchers told me that her DNA was too fractured with mixed gender descent and wouldn't be any use to the process of identification. They needed to obtain either a direct male lineage DNA sample or, even better, a direct female lineage sample because it would contain the vital mitochondrial DNA factor that is the strongest defining indicator on bones so old.

I felt completely deflated. I had no idea whether descendants meeting the profile even existed, and if they did, where on earth would someone like me begin searching for them? In a state of total despair, I was lucky enough to come across Tim Lycett, an amazingly dedicated researcher with the independent Fromelles Descendant Database team. Tim and his project partner, Sandra Playle, had been looking for the families of these missing men and building portraits of their lives on an entirely voluntary basis. They were so incredibly committed to the work even though neither of them had a relative directly involved. They were a huge inspiration to me.

Tim played a vital role in guiding me through my family history. He let me bombard him with all my information and genuinely shared my excitement when I finally had a breakthrough.

When I was a little girl, my grandmother Vivienne used to tell me stories about the Jentsches. She was the youngest child of Rosalia Emily, and only four years old when her mother died of tuberculosis at the age of forty-three. Apparently, her mother's sister, Milly, wanted to take the motherless children and raise them as her own, and this caused a rift with Nanna's widowed father and the Jentsch family. Even though Nanna didn't have much contact with the Jentsches after that, her big sister, who was eleven years older than her, clearly recalled spending time with their mother's family before their mother died and would speak about them often. Now, as an adult, I could understand the strong bond that Nanna felt with them through the mother she lost when she was very young.

Nanna had been diagnosed with Alzheimer's disease quite some time previously and as the years went by it was heartbreaking to witness her memory slipping away. All I know is that if she'd had the ability to understand there was a good chance Ernest's remains might be discovered, she would have kept very close tabs on the investigation and no doubt done everything possible to help with the search.

Our family prayer book is one of my most treasured possessions. I remember Nanna collecting clippings and notices from the local papers about newsworthy family events and pasting them carefully into its pages. The book was started by Nanna's mother, Rosalia. It was her Anglican prayer book. After Rosalia's untimely death, Nanna's big sister, who was called Rosalie, continued the tradition of pasting family notices in its pages until her death in 1972, when Nanna took over the task. Almost 120 years of articles have been passed down through the generations of my family, and now it's entrusted to my keeping. Full of wonderful stories and memories, it also held vital clues in our search for Ernest and proved to be an invaluable resource.

Ernest had a brother and sister but no direct descendants. His brother had died as an infant, and although his sister married and lived a long and happy life, she had no children. Knowing that there was no DNA match to be found along this route, I decided the best option was to find a descendant from the mother's side of Ernest's family, as the mitochondrial DNA was more conclusive and would provide a greater chance of a match.

I began by contacting the Australian War Memorial, where the photograph of Ernest was held in its archives. The file said someone named D. Beckman had donated it from the estate of Ernest's sister shortly after her death in 1993. I felt sure that this person must somehow be related and was eager to find him/her. However, the treasure trove of memorabilia I uncovered in the archives was totally unexpected. Along with the photograph of Ernest were his service medals, the identity disc taken from his body and later returned to the family by the Germans, a sweetheart badge, a mother's badge that had presumably belonged to Alice, his Temperance Society medallion, a scroll and finally his death plaque.

The joy of this discovery was rather spoiled by my first frustrating encounter with privacy legislation. Even though I made it very clear that the identification of a long-missing digger was at stake, the staff at the Australian War Memorial were duty bound not to reveal any personal details of the elusive Beckman who had donated the items. All they could tell me was that the donation was from New South Wales.

In sheer desperation, I picked up the telephone book and began to ring as many Beckmans as possible. After explaining my motives over and over again to dozens of understandably suspicious Beckmans, I decided there had to be another way. I wrote a letter explaining that my sole agenda was to have this poor fellow identified and buried with honour, and sent it to over seventy Beckman households throughout New South Wales. Over several weeks, I had many delightful telephone conversations with people from these families wishing me well in my quest. Sadly, none were the D. Beckman I was looking for.

In the end, I went back to the Australian War Memorial begging for help, and they agreed to make an approach to the donor on my behalf. The result was disappointing. It appeared that D. Beckman had passed away some time ago and his widow was totally unaware of the donation he had made. In fact, she was adamant that there was no connection between her husband's family and Ernest whatsoever.

To this day, I still don't know how Mr Beckman came to be in possession of our family's precious collection, and I doubt that I will ever know the truth. Nevertheless, I will always be indebted to him for having the decency to pass it on to the Australian War Memorial, where all current and future generations of my family will have the opportunity to view it.

I was back to square one again.

At this point, I turned to the family prayer book. Using information gathered from years of newspaper clippings and comparing them with births, deaths and marriages archives, I worked out that Ernest's mother, Alice, was one of four sisters. Surely, I thought, there must be someone living from one of those families with the vital mitochondrial link. But once again the privacy laws thwarted my attempts to trace the families of the three sisters. In the end, I went back to the telephone, wrote more letters, scanned archives at the New South Wales State Library, placed notices in newspapers and joined various online forums. No joy.

Down but not out, I felt it was time to hunt for a paternal descendant through the family of Ernest's father – the Jentsches. I was fortunate enough to discover some information from family-history websites and received a great deal of help from Barry Konemann, a distant cousin whom I met online. He had been working through the Jentsch family tree for several years and helped me to piece together the puzzle, providing several leads to help me find the elusive paternal DNA match.

As time marched on and the deadline approached for the family-tree submissions, I began to panic. I knew no one I'd encountered was a suitable match to Ernest because, like me, they all had a fractured DNA lineage. Despite assurances from the Fromelles Project Group that I had plenty of time and Tim Lycett urging me to keep plugging away, I began to feel that I was letting Ernest and his family down. By this stage, I had developed a deep affection for 'Our Ernest' and, to my embarrassment, I would find myself dissolving into tears whenever I thought of not being able to help him.

The search for Ernest began to take over my life, and it wasn't long before my near and dear ones were rolling their eyes every time I mentioned his name. They understood my passion and happily supported my efforts, but when I started to voice my frustrations directly at Ernest, shouting that he'd better start helping me if he wanted to get found, they began to wonder if I was just a little bit obsessed. I have to admit I was.

The more I researched, the more I began to feel a 'connection' to this distant relative of mine. I found out that Ernest came close to death after a tram accident in Sydney when he was a child. I found out that he worked as a clerk at the Tooth brewery, which was surprisingly at odds with his Temperance Society medallion. But what most struck a chord with me was the revelation that he had a deep and abiding love of motorcycles. I would imagine him gazing at the gleaming new Triumphs in the dealership close to his workplace, and I knew exactly how he felt because, in an extraordinary coincidence, my husband and I both share the same passion. At one stage, we even owned a motorcycle shop that was stocked with a large selection of our beloved Triumphs.

Then, in September 2009, came the breakthrough. I had tracked down a young man named Michael Jentsch and found myself speaking with his father, Peter, who had just returned from a trip to Germany and Poland with his father, tracing the Jentsch family roots in Saxony. We shared the history of our respective family lines and located where our distant generations merged. As Peter explained his family tree, my excitement grew. Could it be true? Could he be the one? It took a number of minutes and many questions for the facts to establish themselves, but in the end there was no doubt in my mind – Peter and his father were the direct paternal line to Ernest that we so desperately needed.

In floods of tears, I burst through the door of my parents' home. They, of course, thought that something terrible had happened, until I managed to explain through sobs of joy that

I had found the Jentsches. They knew how much this meant to me and were equally ecstatic at the news. I hadn't anticipated such an emotional reaction, but it was getting clear to me that, in a strange way, Ernest had come to feel like my own child. I had somehow inherited the responsibility of rekindling and honouring his memory, along with the living breath of hope left behind by his bereaved parents.

With Peter's information, I was finally able to complete the family tree and submit it to the Fromelles Project Group in time. It was now up to the experts to decide whether Peter and his father were suitable candidates for DNA matching. I felt quietly confident that they were our best chance.

A month later, Peter and his father, John, met me at the Australian War Memorial. Together, we had organised a viewing of the items belonging to Ernest that had been donated by Mr Beckman. The afternoon I spent with the two men who shared the same building blocks of life as Ernest was incredibly moving. I held the identity disc that Ernest was wearing when he died, and felt transported to another place and time. Though light in my hand, the disc weighed heavily on my heart as I contemplated what these young boys had endured. War can never be the best solution to the world's complaints, but that doesn't diminish the deeds and sacrifices made by those who have it thrust upon them.

More positive news was to follow. Some weeks after the Australian War Memorial visit, I was contacted online by the family of Ernest's aunt. They in turn put me in touch with the sons of Ernest's cousin, Beryl Salmon, whose brother Harold had also been killed during the Great War. Ken and Roy Brown had never heard about Ernest, but when they were told that they potentially possessed the precious maternal mitochondrial link, they were more than happy to assist.

So now we had both paternal and maternal DNA links to Ernest, and I knew that if he really was one of those recovered from the mass graves at Pheasant Wood and reburied in the newly constructed Commonwealth War Graves cemetery nearby, then his chance of being identified was better than ever. All we had to do was await the final testing and results from the sitting of the first identification committee. I found myself muttering to Ernest over and over again, 'Hang in there, mate, we're only a DNA test away from finding you.'

At 11.10 a.m. on 16 March 2010, my phone rang. It was a representative from the Fromelles Project Group. Ernest had been identified.

Alongside the births of my three children, it was a high point of my life. The tears rolled down my cheeks and I whooped with joy. Babbling my thanks to the poor man on the phone (who I'm sure I had temporarily deafened), I finally hung up. In the brief silence that followed, I took a moment to think of the mother who had died not knowing where her son lay. I felt an enormous amount of pride and immense gratitude to all those who had played a part in helping me find Ernest. A son torn from his parents and lost in battle all those years ago had now been found and returned to the embrace of his family.

Meanwhile, my grandmother's health had been steadily declining and we were advised by the medicos that she didn't have long. I put together a collage of family portraits for her, and she would point out the photo of herself as a little girl alongside her mother and even spark up somewhat at the mention of the name Jentsch. Some days, I would sit with her and patiently describe every new development in the search for Ernest. There were times when I looked into her eyes and felt sure she understood exactly what I was saying, but as her condition progressively worsened these moments became few and far between. The day finally arrived when our reluctance to lose her was outweighed by my grandmother's right to dignity, and we quietly whispered to her that it was all right to go. Yet, grasping on to life, she steadfastly refused, telling us over and over again that she was 'waiting'.

When Ernest's identification came through, I visited Nanna to tell her the news. Through tears of happiness and sorrow, I asked her to say hello to Ernie for me. She passed away the following day.

On Mother's Day 2010, I went to the Northern Suburbs Crematorium and placed a bouquet of flowers at the final resting place of Alice Jentsch. I also left a note telling her that her boy had finally been found. It was something I felt I needed to do for both her and Ernest. I walked away grateful in the knowledge that she could now rest peacefully.

Nominated by the entire family as their representative, I was given the daunting task of composing the epitaph to be inscribed on Ernest's headstone. I wanted to echo the words of his parents but still comply with the strict criteria laid out by the Commonwealth War Graves Commission, so I searched for inspiration in the memorial notices that the Jentsch family had placed in the newspapers every year since 1935. With plenty of family input, we settled on words we believe best express our own feelings and those of his parents:

Our Beloved Son, Ernest
Dear Brother of Muriel
Tho' Great Seas Divide Us
His Memory Will Ever Last

In July 2010 my parents and I, along with two distant cousins, Barry Konemann and John Chapman, travelled to France for the dedication ceremony of the new Fromelles (Pheasant Wood) Military Cemetery. On the ninety-fourth anniversary of the battle, a large group assembled, including Charles, Prince of Wales, and Her Excellency Governor General of Australia Quentin Bryce. Hundreds of descendants were there to pay their respects to the missing men. Watching from temporary stands as the final unknown soldier was interred next to Ernest, I felt a tremendous sense of honour to be representing all the generations of Ernest's family.

Later, after all the pomp and ceremony had finished and much of the world's media had gone away, the families of the ninety-six identified men were given their first opportunity to access the cemetery itself. It was the moment I had dreamed of.

I must have sprinted to Ernest's grave because suddenly it was there in front of me. Seeing his headstone for that first time, I contained myself just long enough to lean over and place the flowers as promised to Alice, before I fell to my knees and wept uncontrollably for the loss of this dear boy. I felt the comforting arm of my mother settling around my shoulders and leaned in to her, only to realise I was actually being held in the consoling embrace of the governor general. I tried to explain my outburst, but I could tell I was hardly making sense. I needn't have worried, for her warm compassion and silent empathy reassured me that I was not alone.

Fortunately, my parents caught up to us at that moment and engaged Her Excellency in conversation while I tried to compose myself. The governor general spent the next fifteen minutes listening intently as we told her Ernest's story and how he finally came to be found.

Later, at a private ceremony conducted by a clergyman at Ernest's graveside, I gave a reading from my great-grandmother's prayer book. Then I walked through the cemetery looking at all the other headstones of soldiers whose names were so familiar. Over the years, I had devoured every skerrick of information about the '19th of July' boys, and I knew most of their stories. It felt so right that they were reunited and finally honoured as they deserved to be.

We returned to Fromelles the next day to visit Ernest one last time. After a while, the rest of my family walked back into the village but I found that I just couldn't leave. I sat on the cool lawn beside his grave and tried to imagine what it must have been like when Ernest was there in 1916. A wasteland of misery and suffering, far from the serene and beautiful place it is today. I was glad to spend that tranquil time alone with 'my Ernest' and took enormous pleasure in knowing that, after ninety-four years, he was finally resting in peace.

Ernest continues to be in my thoughts every day. His photograph is on my fridge and in my wallet along with those of my children, grandchild, niece and nephews. He is my hero, and I can honestly say that, even though I never met him, I love him dearly. As long as I am alive, his memory will endure and be honoured.

Recently, my youngest son and I bought a model of a 1908 vintage motorcycle. We have decided that this year we will put it under our Christmas tree . . . for Ernie.

Annette Darling Tebb

Appendix

THE FACES OF
PHEASANT WOOD

Of the 250 soldiers recovered from Pheasant Wood, 124 have been identified so far, all Australians. With the willing assistance of descendants and through detailed research, we have been able to locate photographs for 97 of this number. Their details appear below.

ARNOTT, Colin, 1968 Private, 30th Battalion

BARBER, William, 346 Private, 32nd Battalion

BENNETT, Allan, 1602 Lance Corporal, 32nd Battalion

BISHOP, Raymond, 3761 Private, 55th Battalion

BOLT, Herbert, 3009 Corporal, 55th Battalion

BOURKE, Harold, 1682 Private, 30th Battalion

BROADHURST, Leonard, 3013 Private, 55th Battalion

BRUMM, Norman, 1470 Private, 29th Battalion

BURNEY, Edward, 1226 Private, 32nd Battalion

BURNS, Robert, Lieutenant, 14th Machine Gun Co.

CHINNER, Eric, Lieutenant, 32nd Battalion

CLINGAN, Alexander, 3168 Private, 53rd Battalion

CORIGLIANO, Maurice, 2011 Private, 32nd Battalion

COSGRIFF, Thomas, 2150 Private, 59th Battalion

CRAIGIE, William, 4420 Lance Corporal, 54th Battalion

CRESSY, Henry, 4179A Private, 54th Battalion

CROKER, Harry, 2010 Private, 30th Battalion

CUCKSON, William, 3032 Private, 54th Battalion

CULLEN, William, 623 Private, 31st Battalion

DEWAR, Robert, 3047 Private, 55th Battalion

DIBBEN, Edwin, 4183A Private, 54th Battalion

DUNSTAN, Benedict, 4483 Private, 54th Battalion

DYSON, Fred, 3560A Private, 54th Battalion

ESAM, Harold, 391 Private, 31st Battalion

FARLOW, Samuel, 80 Private, 29th Battalion

FENWICK, Robert, 882 Private, 30th Battalion

FLETCHER, Frederick, 3310 Corporal, 55th Battalion

FORLAND, Robert, 4779 Private, 53rd Battalion

FORREST, John, 3046 Private, 54th Battalion

FRANCIS, Thomas, 2584 Private, 29th Battalion

GOULDING, John, 555 Private, 55th Battalion

GREEN, Robert, 1274 Corporal, 32nd Battalion

GRIFFITHS, Gilbert, 1276 Private, 32nd Battalion

HALE, Norman, 702 Private, 31st Battalion

HARRIOTT, Laurence, 4509 Private, 54th Battalion

HEPPLE, Matthew, 2056 Private, 30th Battalion

HIGGINS, William, 196 Private, 30th Battalion

HOLLIDAY, Clifford, 4801 Private, 54th Battalion

HOLMES, Arnold, 955 Private, 32nd Battalion

IRVIN, David, 4807 Private, 54th Battalion

IRVING, Allan, 1528 Private, 32nd Battalion

JAMIESON, William, 2144 Private, 31st Battalion

JENTSCH, Ernest, 3331 Lance Sergeant, 53rd Battalion

JOHNSTON, Cyril, 4315A Private, 54th Battalion

KENDALL, Hassell, 365 Corporal, 31st Battalion

LAWLOR, Daniel, 126 Private, 32nd Battalion

LEISTER, Leslie, 4840 Private, 55th Battalion

LIVINGSTON, David, 1168 Private, 29th Battalion

MAYER, Henry, 2873 Private, 55th Battalion

McDOWELL, Athol, 3194 Sergeant, 60th Battalion

McKENZIE, Alec, 1797A Private, 32nd Battalion

McKENZIE, John, 151 Private, 32nd Battalion

McLEAN, Hughie, 293 Private, 32nd Battalion

MENDELSOHN, Berrol, Lieutenant, 55th Battalion

MITCHELL, Alan, Lieutenant, 30th Battalion

MOMPLHAIT, Alfred, 3282 Private, 32nd Battalion

MORLEY, John, 258 Private, 31st Battalion (real name: William HOWARD)

NEVILL, Joseph, 269 Private, 31st Battalion

NORRIS, Ignatius, Lieutenant Colonel, 53rd Battalion

PAGAN, George, 2906 Lance Corporal, 54th Battalion

PARKER, John, Lieutenant, 30th Battalion

PARRY, Frederick, 320 Private, 29th Battalion

PFLAUM, Raymond, 161 Private, 32nd Battalion

PHEASANT, Walter, 2462 Private, 54th Battalion

PITT, Harold, 595 Private, 32nd Battalion

POLLARD, Herbert, 324 Private, 29th Battalion

PRATT, Albert, Second Lieutenant, 53rd Battalion

PRETTY, Walter, 1556 Private, 32nd Battalion

RANDALL, Howard, 1558 Private, 32nd Battalion

RAWLINGS, Frederick, 916 Private, 31st Battalion

REID, Maurice, 3256 Private, 32nd Battalion

RIDLER, Samuel, 1036 Private, 32nd Battalion

ROSS, James, 1216 Corporal, 29th Battalion

RUSSELL, Arthur, 4299 Private, 54th Battalion

RYAN, Daniel, 743 Private, 30th Battalion

SAMPSON, Victor, Major, 53rd Battalion

SCOTT, Robert, 1046 Private, 32nd Battalion

SHERIDAN, Thomas, Captain, 29th Battalion

SIMON, Victor, 1516 Private, 32nd Battalion

SPENCE, Malcolm, 4614 Private, 30th Battalion

STALGIS, Gregory, 2898 Corporal, 14th Machine Gun Co.

STEAD, Joseph, 187 Private, 32nd Battalion

STEED, Frank, 755 Corporal, 30th Battalion

TUCK, Alfred, 1252 Corporal, 29th Battalion

TUCKER, William, 1581 Private, 32nd Battalion

TURNER, John, 767 Private, 30th Battalion

VERPILLOT, Aime', 4885 Private, 53rd Battalion

VINCENT, Laurence, 777 Private, 30th Battalion

WARD, Claude, 2184 Private, 30th Battalion

WEBB, Thomas, 2910 Private, 60th Battalion

WEIR, Arthur, 358 Private, 29th Battalion

WILDMAN, Reginald, 1888 Private, 54th Battalion (real name: Reginald BRADNEY)

WILKIN, Ernest, 1314 Private, 29th Battalion

WILLIS, Henry, 983 Private, 31st Battalion

WILSON, Eric, 4887 Private, 53rd Battalion
WILSON, Samuel, 3534 Private, 53rd Battalion
WYNN, John, 2485 Private, 30th Battalion

For the remaining 27 soldiers, we continue to search for their images and until then remember their names below:

BALKIN, Michael, 4254 Private, 54th Battalion
BARRETT, Rossiter, 3031 Private, 55th Battalion
BENSON, George, 840 Private, 30th Battalion
BILLS, Thomas Henry, 605 Private, 31st Battalion
BROMLEY, Albert, 4744 Private, 53rd Battalion
CROFT, George, 2006 Private, 30th Battalion
FAHEY, Patrick, 3060 Private, 55th Battalion
GEASON, Percy, 4811 Private, 55th Battalion
HART, Leslie, 865 Corporal, 32nd Battalion
HASLAM, Herbert, 1390 Private, 29th Battalion
HAWCROFT, Charles, 188 Private, 30th Battalion
HUNGERFORD, George, 3327 Private, 53rd Battalion
JAMES, Frederick, 3347 Private, 14th Machine Gun Company
JOHNSON, Arthur, 2203 Private, 29th Battalion
LOADER, Frank, 2064 Private, 32nd Battalion
LUCRE, George, 467 Private, 30th Battalion
MOORE, William, 3393 Private, 53rd Battalion
MOREY, Gilbert, 3366 Private, 53rd Battalion
MORGAN, Cecil, 2055 Private, 31st Battalion (real name: Colin MEYERS)
MURRAY, Charles, 1590 Corporal, 30th Battalion
O'DONNELL, William, 319 Private, 32nd Battalion
REID, James, 335 Sergeant, 29th Battalion
RONSON, William, 3102 Private, 53rd Battalion
RYAN, Daniel, 743 Private, 30th Battalion
TISBURY, Charles, 1623 Private, 30th Battalion
WALLIS, Joseph, 4617 Private, 54th Battalion
WALSH, Leslie, 311 Private, 31st Battalion

BIBLIOGRAPHY

BOOKS

Austin, R., *Black and Gold: The History of the 29th Battalion 1915–1918*, Slouch Hat Publications, Melbourne, 1997

Bean, C. E. W., *Anzac to Amiens*, Australian War Memorial, Canberra, 1946

Bean, C. E. W., *Official History of Australia in the War, 1914– 1918, Volume III*, Queensland University Press, St Lucia, Queensland, 1982

Burla, B., *Crossed Boomerangs: A History of all the 31st Battalions*, Australian Military History Publications, Loftus, New South Wales, 2005

Corfield, R., *Don't Forget Me Cobber*, Miegunyah Press, Melbourne, 2009

Downing, W. H., *To the Last Ridge*, Duffy and Snellgrove, Potts Point NSW, 1998

Ellis, Capt. A. D., *The Story of the Fifth Australian Division*, Hodder and Stoughton, London, 1920

Freeman, R., *Second to None: A Memorial History of the 32nd Battalion AIF*, Peacock Publications, Norwood, South Australia, 2006

Kennedy, J. J., *The Whale Oil Guards*, The Naval and Military Press, Uckfield, East Sussex, 2009

Knyvett, Capt. R. H., *Over There with the Australians*, Charles
    Scribner's Sons, New York, 1918

Lavis, J., *Theodor Pflaum's War Diary*, J. Lavis, North
    Adelaide, 2002

Lindsay, P., *Fromelles*, Hardie Grant, Melbourne, 2007

McMullin, R., *Pompey Elliott*, Scribe Publications,
    Melbourne, 2002

Pedersen, P., *Fromelles*, Leo Cooper, Barnsley, South
    Yorkshire, 2004

St Claire, R., *Our Gift to the Empire: 54th Australian Infantry
    Battalion 1916–1919*, Ross St Claire, New South Wales,
    2006

Summers, J., *Remembering Fromelles*, Commonwealth War Graves
    Commission, London, 2010

Tiveychoc, A., *There and Back*, Returned Sailors and Soldiers
    Imperial League of Australia, Sydney, 1935

Wilkinson, C., *Fromelles: Australia's Bloodiest Day at War*, Black
    Dog Books, Melbourne, 2011

PAPERS AND COLLECTIONS

Barton, P., 'Report on Research Carried Out in Geneva,
    Munich and Ingolstadt', 2009

Pollard, T., 'Pheasant Wood Fromelles – Data Structure
    Report', G.U.A.R.D. Report 12008, Glasgow
    University, 2008

Whitford, T., 'The Origin and Distribution of the Shire of
    Alberton Medallion 1914–1916', unpublished, 2009

Australian War Memorial

Australian Red Cross Wounded and Missing Enquiry Files:
    www.awm.gov.au/research/people/wounded_and_missing

Australian War Memorial Collection:
www.awm.gov.au/search/collections

Australian War Memorial Roll of Honour:
www.awm.gov.au/research/people/roll_of_honour

National Archives of Australia

Court of Inquiry – to Inquire into and Report upon certain matters in connection with the Australian Graves Service, Series MP367/1, Control Symbol 446/10/1840

Removal of Bodies to Australia – Graves in Germany, Series MP367/1, Control Symbol 446/10/3410

War Service Records, First World War, Series B2455

WEBSITES

Don't Forget Me Cobber:
www.army.gov.au/fromelles

Fromelles Descendant Database:
www.facebook.com/#!/groups/353275321398458

Great War Forum:
http://1914-1918.invisionzone.com

Lest We Forget: The Virtual Australian First World War Museum:
www.lestweforget.com.au

Pheasant Wood: The Lost Diggers of Fromelles:
www.smh.com.au/interactive/2009/national/fromelles

ACKNOWLEDGEMENTS

First and foremost, Sandra and I would like to thank all the researchers who volunteered their time and energy to help us track down the stories of the missing soldiers and their descendants. From all across the globe, their services played a vital role in the Database's success.

Among these fine people we would particularly like to single out the efforts of Roger Freeman, without whose exceptional contribution we could never have come this far; Victoria Burbidge and Melvyn Pack, whose long-distance support from England and ongoing work to identify the missing British soldiers deserves a great deal more recognition; Amanda Taylor, Andrew Pittaway, Bill Wyndham, Carrie Doolan, Dan Irving, David Dial, David Hamilton, Graeme Hosken, Maggie Grenham, Matt Smith, Michelle Leonard, Peter Bennett, Peter Nelson, Ross St Claire, Steve Morse, Terry Bugg and finally the members of both the Great War and Rootschat internet forums.

We are also extremely grateful to the many descendants of the missing Fromelles men who were willing to share delicate personal information about their ancestors and their individual family histories. Without their enthusiasm and encouragement, none of this would have been possible. In particular, we are indebted to Annette Darling Tebb who agreed to make public her very personal journey in the epilogue, Tho' Great Seas Divide Us.

A number of journalists have been conspicuous in their support of our work, helping to promote the research through their newspapers. Many thanks to Bridie Smith of *The Age,* who wrote about our activities and plugged our website whenever possible.

Paola Totaro of the *Sydney Morning Herald* and her husband Robert Wainwright provided sound and positive advice when the Fromelles Descendant Database was in its infancy. Paola deserves our eternal gratitude for her constant promotion of our efforts and for the outstanding interactive website she set up based largely on our research, which received the high honour of being nominated for a Walkley Award for journalism. It was Paola who first planted the idea for a book about 'The Final Chapter' and we hope we've done justice to all that she envisaged for the story.

Our heartfelt appreciation to the 'Families and Friends of the First AIF' and their vice president, Jim Munro. The FFFAIF frequently promoted the Fromelles Descendant Database to its members and Jim was always ready with timely advice, especially when the enormous workload began to take its toll on us.

To our friends Chris and Shirley Durrant, our sincerest thanks for offering suggestions and revisions as the book came together.

Our thanks also go to all the people at Penguin Books who looked beyond the tactics of battle and recognised the important human tale entwined through generations of Australian families touched by the tragedy of Fromelles. The inspiration and vision of Belinda Byrne and Andrea McNamara, combined with the skilful touch of Jennifer Castles, fuelled our determination to see this project through. Without their patience and courage in taking on a complete novice, this book may never have made it to the printers!

We received immeasurable assistance from the man who started it all: Lambis Englezos. Not only Sandra and I, but also the people of this country owe him an immense debt of gratitude. There can be no praise high enough for the quiet determination and unwavering resolve he displayed in his pursuit of peace and honour for those Australians who died so far from their homes and from the people they loved. To Lambis and Tim Whitford we extend our sincerest gratitude for their ongoing friendship and trust.

It's impossible to express how indebted we feel to our families and in particular Tim's partner, Tracey. Their selfless support in allowing us to indulge our obsession knows no bounds. For that they have our eternal love and thanks.

Finally, to the memory of all those who served Australia during the calamitous years of the Great War, we vow to do everything in our power to ensure you are never forgotten. It's our belief that more than any other nation on earth, Australia fiercely upholds its tradition of remembrance and for this we should all be justly proud.

FROM SANDRA

The Fromelles boys entered into an extremely traumatic period of my life and there are times when I believed they were the reason for guiding me through it; therefore, the title *Fromelles: The Final Chapters* has personal significance for me.

Many wonderful people contribute to the success of books and this one is successful due to the dedication of my very good friend Tim Lycett. I am extremely grateful for the long hours of research and writing that he did on my behalf. Tim did this without question and therefore I must acknowledge the wonderful writing he has done for the book. I must thank Tim's wife, Tracey, for all her support and encouragement along the way.

Other people who have answered our call for help, or assisted me personally are:

Amanda Taylor, Andrew Pittaway, Annette Darling Tebb, Bill Wyndham, Blaxhall Archive Group, Bridie Smith, Carolyn Harris, Carrie Doolan, Chris and Shirley Durrant, Dan Irving, David Dial, David Hamilton, Families of the AIF Fromelles soldiers, FFFAIF Inc and members, Glenn Phillips, Graeme Hosken, GUARD, Joseph Catanzaro, Lambis Englezos, Maggie Grenham, Matt Smith, Melvyn Pack, Members of Rootschat.com, Members of the Great War Forum, Michelle Leonard, Paola Totaro, Peter Barton, Peter Bennett, Peter Dennis, Peter Francis, Peter Nelson, Robert Wainwright, Roger Freeman, Ross St Claire, Steve Morse, *Sydney Morning Herald*, Terry Bugg, Tim Whitford, Tony Pollard and Victoria Burbidge. I thank you all so very much.

A special thank you to our families and friends who supported our Fromelles obsession and to the families and descendants who have so willingly offered their time, stories, photographs and family archives to assist in creating a living history of the Fromelles Lads.

Lest we forget!

SOURCES

p.27   *Today I lead my Batallion*: McCrae, Maj. G. G., Private correspondence: AWM 1DRL/0427

p.28   *From the line of lights*: Ellis, Capt. A. D., *The Story of the Fifth Australian Division* (1920)

p.29–30 *We soon began to discover*: Knyvett, Capt. R. H., *Over There with the Australians* (1918)

p.36   *He told me that our fellers*: Lavis, J., *Theodor Pflaum's War Diary* (2002)

p.37   *He was lying wounded*: Green, 1274 Cpl. R. C., Red Cross Wounded and Missing Enquiry Bureau Files, AWM 1DRL/0428

p.40   *You no doubt have heard*: Hardy, Lt. F., Private correspondence

p.40   *He was in my platoon*: Green, 1274 Cpl. R. C., Red Cross Wounded and Missing Enquiry Bureau Files, AWM 1DRL/0428

p.41   *I am writing this in the morning*: Elliott, Brig. Gen. H. E., Private correspondence, AWM 2DRL/513/7-9

p.42   *Boys, you won't find*: Bean, C. E. W., *Official History of Australia in the War 1914–1918*, Volume III (1982)

p.43   *The trenches are full*: 15th Brigade War Diary, AWM 4/23/15/5

p.46   *Scores of stammering German machine guns*: Downing, W. H., *To the Last Ridge* (1998)

p.46   *The first wave went down*: Knyvett, Capt. R. H., *Over There with the Australians* (1918)

p.48   *61st Division not attacking tonight*: 15th Brigade War Diary, AWM
        4/23/15/5

p.49   *Come on lads!*: Saint Ignatius College, Riverview NSW, *Our Alma
        Mater* (1916)

p.49   *Your dear husband*: Kennedy, Chaplain J. J., Private correspondence

p.52   *As I lay in McDonald's arms*: Ridley, Lt. J. G., Private correspondence:
        AWM 2DRL/0775

p.55   *Pompey got tired of sitting*: Schroeder, Capt. J. D., Private
        correspondence: AWM38 3DRL 606/276

p.56   *The scene in the Australian trenches*: Bean, C. E. W., *Anzac to Amiens*
        (1946)

p.56   *I think the attack*: Haking, Lt. Gen. Sir., XI Corps Report (1916)

p.56   *Yesterday evening, south of Armentières*: Official British Army
        Communiqué/Press Release

p.59   *We found a man*: Knyvett, Capt. R. H., *Over There With The Australians*
        (1918)

p.60   *We found a fine haul*: Fraser, 3101 Sgt. S., Private correspondence,
        AWM 1DRL/0300

p.62   *We found the old No-man's land*: Bean, C. E. W., Diaries and
        Notebooks, AWM 3RDL/606/117/1

p.63   *The English bodies*: Von Braun, Maj. Gen. J. R., 6th Bavarian Reserve
        Division, List of English military personnel buried in the area held by
        this Division, Munich Archives

p.64   *The removal of effects*: Ibid.

p.65   *The misappropriation of even the most*: Ibid.

p.66   *To my horror*: Barry, W. C., Private correspondence, AWM PR00814

p.67   *I was nearly demented*: Pearson A. (Nancie), Private correspondence

p.69   *I had a letter from the Red Cross*: Pearson A. (Nancie), Private
        correspondence

p.68   *Perhaps they can't find the dear boys remains*: Pearson, A. (Nancie),
        Private correspondence

p.70–1   *While the men were getting*: Lavis, J., *Theodor Pflaum's War Diary* (2002)

p.71–2   *On July 20th last year*: Pflaum, 161 Private R. H., War Service Record, NAA B2455

p.72   *and in reply to state*: Ibid.

p.73–4   *He once told me*: Pflaum, H.A.T., Private correspondence: AWM PR86/114

p.75–6   *Intelligence Officer, at chief army command*: Red Cross Wounded and Missing Enquiry Bureau Files, AWM 1DRL/0428 and War Service Records, NAA B2455

p.76   *Missing since July 20th*: Irving, 1528 Private A. W. J., War Service Record, NAA B2455

p.79   *From this it can only be assumed*: Holliday, 4801 Private C. D., War Service Record, NAA B2455

p.80   *Had we been told on 9th August*: Ibid.

p.80–1   *This may, we fear*: Ibid.

p.81   *It is abundantly clear*: Ibid.

p.81–2   *You are advised that*: Ibid.

p.83   *After the battle near Fromelles*: Bowden, 2nd Lt. J., Red Cross Wounded and Missing Enquiry Bureau Files, AWM 1DRL/0428

p.85   *For God's sake have it carried out*: Court of Inquiry – to Inquire into and Report upon certain matters in connection with the Australian Graves Service, NAA MP367/1

p.85–6   *The records in Australia House*: Ibid.

p.86–7   *I carried out a personal search*: Ibid.

p.88   *A born leader of men*: Defence. Graves. Visit of Mr [Stanley Melbourne] Bruce, NAA A458

p.88–9   *Opportunity for abuse is great*: Court of Inquiry – to Inquire into and Report upon certain matters in connection with the Australian Graves Service, NAA MP367/1

p.97   *In one of five large British collective graves*: Bowden, 2nd Lt. J., Red Cross Wounded and Missing Enquiry Bureau Files, AWM 1DRL/0428 p.97   *Every one of those names*: Lindsay, P., *Fromelles* (2007)

p.100   *Casualties of the battle*: 16th Bavarian Reserve Infantry Regiment - Unit History, Photographer Hans Bauer

p.102   *The Panel was of the view that*: Fromelles Panel of Investigation, August 2005

p.107   *The bodies of English soldiers*: Von Braun, Maj. Gen. J. R., 6th Bavarian Reserve Division, *List of English military personnel buried in the area held by this Division*, Kriegsarchiv [War Archive] Munich

p.107   *For the enemy dead*: 21st Bavarian Reserve Infantry Regiment War Diary, Kriegsarchiv [War Archive] Munich

p.114   *2 November 1915*: *Gippsland Standard* newspaper, February 1920, National Archives of Australia, mfm NX 522

p.115   *The undersigned would be pleased*: *Gippsland Standard* newspaper, November 1915-May 1916, National Archives of Australia, mfm NX 522

p.115-6 *I have not yet received*: *Gippsland Standard* newspaper, March 1920, National Archives of Australia, mfm NX 522

p.116   Four of my sons received: Ibid.

p.118   *This is all the information*: Lear, 4130 Private I. J., War Service Record, NAA B2455

p.123   *We don't always have the capacity*: AM, ABC Radio, 1st October 2008

p.130   *I had a son named Samuel*: Mellor, 1709 Private S., War Service Record, NAA B2455

p.140   *Knocked about a lot*: Dewar, 3047 Private R. A., Red Cross Wounded and Missing Enquiry Bureau Files, AWM 1DRL/0428

p.141   *Having enlisted tonight*: Aime Constant Verpillot Naturalization, NAA A1/1915/14267

p.141   *I am quite well*: Verpillot, 4885 Private A. C., Private correspondence

p.145-6 *I must say that I have been given*: Great War Forum, www.1914-1918. invisionzone.com/forums

p.156   *The Australian Private Scott*: Scott, 1046 Private R. G. M., Red Cross Wounded and Missing Enquiry Bureau Files, AWM 1DRL/0428 p.156   *The cross will in due course*: Scott, 1046 Private R. G. M., War Service Record, NAA B2455

p.175   *Gordon, John*: Gordon, 1130 Private J., War Service Record, NAA B2455

p.181   *He was wounded at Fleurbaix*: Leister, 4840 Private L., Red Cross Wounded and Missing Enquiry Bureau Files, AWM 1DRL/0428

p.192–3 *Dear Mr Johnson*: Removal of bodies to Australia – Graves in Germany, NAA MP367/1/446/10/3410

p.194   *The moulder, Johann Fischer*: Removal of bodies to Australia – Graves in Germany, NAA MP367/1/446/10/3410

p.194   *I have now to inform you*: Johnson, 715 L/Cpl. R., War Service Record, NAA B2455

p.203   *On 19th July at Fleurbaix*: Dyson, 3560 Private F., Red Cross Wounded and Missing Enquiry Bureau Files, AWM 1DRL/0428

p.207   *He was bombing Germans in a trench*: Wilson, 3534 Private S. C., Red Cross Wounded and Missing Enquiry Bureau Files, AWM 1DRL/0428

p.208   *I got the call from the Australian Army*: Lycett, T., file notes/emails/interviews, March 2010

p.208-9 *We had a phone call from Canberra*: Ibid.

p.209   *I am absolutely ecstatic*: Sydney Morning Herald, 24th April 2010

p.210   *I remember my grandmother*: Lycett, T., file notes/emails/interviews, March 2010

p.210   You have all these defence mechanisms: Ibid.

p.214   *I have been trying to be patient*: Goulding, 555 Private J. J., War Service Record, NAA B2455

p.220   *On the night of 17th/18th*: First World War Diaries, AWM4, 23/63/18 - 46th Infantry Battalion

INDEX